I COUNT—YOU COUNT

The "Do It Ourselves" Marriage Counseling and Enrichment Book

by George Calden, Ph.D.

Foreword by David R. Mace, Ph.D.

ARGUS COMMUNICATIONS
Niles, Illinois

Cover design and book illustration
by Gene Tarpey

FIRST EDITION

Printed in the United States of America

ARGUS COMMUNICATIONS
7440 Natchez Avenue
Niles, Illinois 60648

International Standard Book Number: 0-913592-64-1
Library of Congress Number: 76-7235

2 3 4 5 6 7 8 9 0

Contents

FOREWORD

Our country, in its two hundred years, has achieved much of which we may be proud. But there is one aspect of American life which brings satisfaction to no one. Our divorce rate is currently higher than it has ever been before, and higher than that of any other country in the world that keeps records. Each year, two million American men and women have to admit to failure in the closest of all human relationships.

If we ask why this should be, many explanations could be offered. Today, people are expecting more from marriage than ever before. Ernest Burgess, the "father" of American family sociologists, has told us that what modern husbands and wives want in marriage is a warm, intimate companionship and that they will not settle for less. In the past, under social and religious pressure, married people put up with shallow and unrewarding relationships. No longer will they do so. Marriages can no longer be held together by external coercion. They must be held together by internal cohesion.

This means that married couples must be trained in what we now call "interpersonal competence." It does not just "come naturally." And the most important of all the skills necessary for successful companionship marriage is effective communication.

The Family Service Association of America, in a major four-year study of the causes of marriage failure across the continent, found that deficient communication occurred twice as often as any other factor. Sex problems, money problems, parenthood problems were all far less significant in creating trouble for husbands and wives than communication difficulties. Indeed, it was inability to communicate about these other problems that usually prevented the couple from solving them.

Fortunately, today we are rapidly learning a great deal about couple communication. Important studies are going ahead, and experimental training courses are being offered. But we have some forty-five million married couples in America, and most of them have not yet even heard of this progress. Even if they have, what they are likely to pick up through the news media cannot really touch their lives. There must be a way to get this vital information to where it is needed.

There *is* a way. It can be done through books. But not technical books, and not mere information-giving books. People do not learn much about communication by hearing about it. They must try it out, experiment with it. They must exchange their present ineffective patterns for more effective patterns. They can only do this experimentally and under the guidance of a skilled teacher. How can this be achieved on a scale large enough to make a difference?

I am excited about George Calden's book because he has shown us one way of doing it. This isn't just a book to *read*. It is a book that can guide a married couple together into a new and better relationship. Or several married couples can work through it together. Very skillfully, it provides them with all they need for the task. The author is with them, step by step, as their trainer and counselor.

This book can also be a boon to many marriage counselors. Professional people in these days are often overwhelmed by couples with marriage problems. It is necessary to devote precious time to explaining the elementary principles of communication to these unhappy husbands and wives, because counseling cannot make much headway until the blocked channels of communication have been opened. By giving this book to the couple to work through at home, the basic work could be done outside the counseling office, setting the counselor free to use counseling time for the treatment of deeper and more complex problems.

George Calden is a professional counselor with long years of experience behind him. He is well versed in the dynamics of marital interaction. But that alone is not enough—many people with vast knowledge are not articulate when they try to reach the man in the street. In addition to his knowledge about communication, George Calden is himself a highly effective communicator. I have been impressed by the skill with which he has put his book together. There is nothing in it that the average husband and wife cannot understand. Just the right amount of repetition ensures that they clearly grasp each step before moving on to the next. The author adroitly combines the fruits of the most up-to-date scientific knowledge with the lore of ancient wisdom and the realities of everyday life in our complex world.

To the husband and wife who will use this book as it was meant to be used, much is offered. Suppose you devote three hours to each of the eight sessions—the equivalent of one day in your lives. With this expenditure of time, if you use it wisely, your life together will begin to move up to a new and higher level. You could start a process of change that would in the end greatly increase the fulfillment you get from, and give to, each other.

David R. Mace
Co-founder, Association of Couples
for Marriage Enrichment (ACME), Inc.

ACKNOWLEDGMENTS

I am deeply indebted:

To the many women and men I've counseled. By letting me share their hurts, struggles, and hopes for happiness, they have deepened my appreciation of the need for improved communication between couples. They have been the major contributors to this book. Most of the dialogues are theirs.

To David Mace and Virginia Satir, whose writings had a major influence on my thinking.

To Jane and Ben Tybring, who introduced my wife and me to the Minnesota Couples Communication Program. Our participation in this program was extremely helpful in clarifying many of my views.

To Felice Bassuk, Bryna Donaldson, and my psychology colleagues, Mary Gutmann and Bill Jackson, who have made a number of valuable suggestions.

To my daughter, Martha, for her sense of humor and her cartoons.

Above all, I am grateful to Ruth, my wife, companion, and counselor, who, for twenty-five enriching years, has made I COUNT—YOU COUNT a reality.

INTRODUCTION
Before you begin

On the day you said, "I do," did you add, "And I also promise to ignore you, tune you out, and take you for granted"? Did your partner respond, "And I promise to nag, argue, distort your remarks, and put you down"?

No couple sets out on a deliberate campaign to communicate poorly. And yet, many lives unfold as if these ridiculous "vows" were actually made.

Do you remember that wonderful spirit of I COUNT—YOU COUNT when you first chose each other as life companions? You still dream of rekindling that feeling. You yearn for intimacy. You want to converse, share affection, have fun, and relax in each other's company. But unfortunately, you have let yourself be swept along by the pressures of daily living, so that you feel straightjacketed by your job or tied down by family chores. As a result, you have allowed very little time for the most precious part of your lives—each other.

Or you may find yourselves behaving more and more like clumsy porcupines trying to make love. When you try to get close, you jab one another. When you are apart, you feel alone and rejected; you feel that I DON'T COUNT.

We all know that communication is at the very heart of a good relationship. Writers repeatedly urge us to communicate if we wish to translate the cold prose of our marriage into warm poetry. But communication is like the weather. It is something we all complain about, but practically no one has worked out specific ways of doing something about it.

The aim of this book is to help you to *do something* about improving your communication.

Marriage: I COUNT—YOU COUNT is a first. It is a self-help, "do-it-ourselves," marriage communication and counseling book, designed for married couples or for any other two adults who wish to enrich their relationship.

The book's major emphasis is on *doing,* on experiencing the joys of intimacy, and on practicing the skills of good communication. I am a strong believer in the old Chinese proverb, "To hear is to forget. To see is to remember. To do is to understand." One picture may be worth a thousand words, but one experience is worth many pictures.

The poet Gibran must have had similar thoughts in mind when he wrote, "A little knowledge that acts is worth infinitely more than much knowledge that is idle."

Marriage: I COUNT—YOU COUNT is unlike most books that are read and appreciated but whose ideas are rarely applied. You may enjoy reading about the pleasures of sitting close, talking to each other, and transmitting warm feelings. But unless you actually live it (as you will in this program), the printed word will have little lasting value.

You and your partner experience the program *together.* Communication, like dancing and making love, involves two people in close touch with one another. Reading the book alone, without your partner's active participation, will be interesting. But you will benefit most when you share the many activities and discussions.

The most distinctive feature of this book is that it offers an actual marriage counseling program. Rather than concentrating on dispensing information, advice, or detailed case histories, *Marriage: I COUNT—YOU COUNT* provides you and your partner with many opportunities for exploring your personal problems and for expressing intimate thoughts. You will be encouraged to tune in to your own feelings, as well as those of your partner, and to share them in a nonthreatening way.

This book was written for you if you have a workable marriage but sense that your life together is far from giving you full satisfaction. *Marriage: I COUNT—YOU COUNT* is for you if you want more from your marriage than just "settling down" and inching along in first or second gear. Improved communication can add a new dimension to your lives.

The book is also intended for those of you who are unhappy about your relationship and are obtaining help from a psychologist, psychiatrist, social worker, marriage counselor, or clergyman. If you belong to this second group, *Marriage: I COUNT—YOU COUNT* can be used as a rewarding adjunct to your counseling. Concurrently with your scheduled visits, you and your partner can share the program at home, or you can meet just before or immediately after your counseling sessions.

You can derive the greatest benefit from the book, however, if your counselor joins you as an active guide during regular counseling sessions. In this sense, the book is like a self-help instruction method for the guitar. You can work on your own, but an instructor can greatly enhance your progress as you go through the manual together.

Although *Marriage: I COUNT—YOU COUNT* is oriented mainly toward individual couples like you and your partner, the two of you may prefer to get together with another couple and experience the program with them.

The book also can easily be adapted for use by small groups of three to six couples. Marriage counselors, leaders of marriage enrichment retreats and marital growth workshops, as well as teachers of marriage and family living courses will find that the program will fit in well with their goals of educating and helping couples to realize their untapped potential.

What can you expect from the program?

There are three participants in this program—you, your partner, and I. I am your author-counselor. I will not be with you in person, but my ideas and suggestions will guide you throughout most of the book. If you are sharing the book with your own counselor, your progress will be greatly enhanced by his or her counseling skills.

If you and your partner are about to go through the book by yourselves, you may wonder whether it is possible to improve your marriage without the direct intervention of a professionally trained person.

In regard to this question, you may be interested in knowing that over 200 couples participated in *Marriage: I COUNT—YOU COUNT* prior to its publication. Half of these couples were referred to me and my colleagues for marriage counseling. The other half consisted of married friends of mine and couples who were participating in church programs and in marriage enrichment groups.

Most of the couples experienced the program entirely on a "do-it-ourselves" basis. Others had minimal assistance from a leader or counselor. The great majority of couples stated that they had benefited considerably from the program. Many of them also offered valuable suggestions for changes in the program. The revisions, based on their comments, helped to facilitate the self-help aspects of the program.

It may help if you think of the program itself as a qualified "counselor" who is assisting and guiding you. But your success, as in professional counseling, will come mainly from your active participation. You will benefit greatly if you are open to new ideas and are willing to try out new ways of speaking and behaving. You are least likely to benefit if you are rigidly set in your ways and if you stubbornly resist change. If you do not have the faintest desire to get along better with your partner, or if you plan to sabotage every effort toward marital betterment, then the book will have little to offer you.

Marriage: I COUNT—YOU COUNT does not guarantee instant happiness. It would be unrealistic to expect all of your problems to evaporate. Also, do not expect the program to make a perfect lady or gentleman out of either of you. As a matter of fact, you may find yourselves letting your feelings out more. Not only will you be able to share your positive attitudes, but you may learn to express your hurt and angry feelings in a more constructive manner.

The program has a number of built-in safeguards aimed at reducing unproductive arguments and destructive squabbles.

What you *can* expect from *Marriage: I COUNT—YOU COUNT* is a fuller appreciation of your own and your partner's inherent self-worth and a real improvement in your ability to understand and respond to one another. The program can help you approach and resolve personal problems before they balloon uncontrollably. Your lives will become enriched as you see and hear each other in new ways.

These days "open marriage," "term marriage," "two-stage" relationships, "I do my thing and you do your thing," and other marriage alternatives are in vogue in some circles. Those who advocate these experimental approaches point to our high divorce rates and loudly announce that marriage, as an institution, has been tried and found wanting. This book takes the opposite attitude. I am convinced that the overwhelming majority of couples ardently *want* marriage. But many have never really *tried* it. They have not given marriage a try by working at it in an open, mature way, guided by the principles of good communication.

Try an I COUNT—YOU COUNT marriage. You'll like it.

A few preliminary instructions

Although this is a planned program, you may be surprised to discover that many of the situations described in these pages are strikingly similar to your own. One wife declared, "They must have been tapping our phone when this book was put together." A number of couples exclaimed, "Hey, that's just like us talking!" You, too, will easily identify with the many dialogues since they are all taken from real-life situations.

You and your partner will be asked to read aloud to one another. Mainly, what you read will reflect how you actually feel. For example, you may read, "I strongly wish to feel self-confident" and recognize it as a desire well known to you. There may be times, however, when the material may not be personally meaningful. When this occurs feel free to skip to the next section. If you are asked to do or say something that you find objectionable, again feel free to skip it and go on. My intention is not to "program" you into talking or behaving in one "true" or "ideal" way. The goal of *Marriage: I COUNT—YOU COUNT* is to encourage you to be yourself; it is meant to be a stimulus to greater openness, not to be manipulative or confining.

The program has eight sessions. It usually takes from one to two hours to complete each session. It may take a bit longer if you read slowly or spend more time in discussion. Several of the sessions may take more time than others. You may prefer to spend two or more meetings on these longer sessions. You may even choose to go through a session twice before going on to the next session. Do not rush through the material. Take your time as you allow the information and experiences to sink in.

Plan to meet weekly on a regularly scheduled basis in complete privacy, away from interruptions. Although once-a-week meetings are preferred, you need not be rigid about this. You may wish to meet twice a week or once every other week. But it should be on a scheduled basis. Otherwise the project will become erratic and unproductive.

As I mentioned, the majority of couples who experienced *Marriage: I COUNT—YOU COUNT* were gratified with the results. A few, unfortunately, did become discouraged because there were no startling breakthroughs after one or two meetings. Others, while happy and even excited over their progress, quit after getting into an argument or after momentarily slipping back into their old, unsatisfying patterns of communication.

The reason I bring this up is to stress the fact that some ups and downs are to be expected. If you were to plot a typical graph of improvement, the chances are it would not be a perfectly straight ascending line. More likely it would resemble a zig-zag line whose general progression is upward. It will be worth your efforts to complete the program. Be patient. You may learn a great deal from your temporary setbacks. Most likely a later session will cover the very problem that troubled you or inhibited your progress.

You should find most of the program quite enjoyable. Improving your communication can be fun, exciting, and adventurous.

For the past twenty years I have worked extensively with couples, as a psychologist, marriage counselor, and family educator. *Marriage: I COUNT—YOU COUNT* is the fruit of these experiences.

Now let's begin.

If I am not for myself, who will be for me?
If I am for myself alone, what am I?
If not now, when?

Hillel

SESSION ONE

Self-worth

You are about to start a journey into intimacy.

If your partner is not near you, call him or her over. Sit close together so that both of you can see the page. It is important to participate together in the reading of this book.

Let's begin by either one of you reading the next paragraph aloud.

(To be read aloud.) *Throughout this program we'll take turns reading each section.* When we see this symbol we will know that it is time for one of us to stop reading and for the other to begin.

We will also notice this symbol: at the beginning of many of the sections. It stands for *shared activity.* It will call our attention to discussion questions or some other activity that we will do *together.* In a few minutes from now we'll be participating in one of these shared activity sections.

And now it's your turn to read the next section aloud.

Self-worth I COUNT

The two words that most often come to mind when we consider how we would like to feel about each other are love and respect. There is a profound but simple truth to these words since they touch upon our most basic psychological need.

It is the need to feel likeable and good about myself.

It is the need for self-worth.

It is the need to feel that I COUNT.

I want to feel like a person, like a somebody. I want to value and respect myself. I dislike feeling small and inadequate.

If we were to think about it, we would be amazed to realize how much of our lives is devoted to maintaining our feelings of self-worth and warding off feelings of inadequacy. We strive to win acceptance from others. We try to improve or hold on to our physical attractiveness. We struggle for success at work. We hope to measure up as good marriage partners. We want to be respected as parents, and we pray that our children will keep out of trouble.

The importance of feeling I COUNT is reflected in the familiar statement of many wives, "I have to be treated like a person before I can respond to you sexually."

We are two uniquely different people. But both of us share the need for self-worth. Both of us strongly wish to feel I COUNT. It can be a great bond between us.

(Now it's your turn to read the next section.)

Our marriage depends a great deal on how strongly each of us feels that I COUNT and that YOU COUNT. As a matter of fact, I cannot think of anything more basic to our relationship than I COUNT—YOU COUNT.

Can you think of anything as important?

In an unhappy marriage there is a LOW COUNT or NO COUNT feeling. We discount each other. We make each other feel small.

In a good marriage, despite the usual disagreements and irritations, there is a high I COUNT and a high YOU COUNT feeling. We help each other grow.

A cynic once said, "Love is a wonderful dream, but marriage is the alarm clock."

A more realistic way of saying this would be, "Love is a wonderful dream, but marriage is the alarm clock when it shatters our I COUNT and YOU COUNT feelings."

Love has been defined in many different ways. Our definition is a simple one:

"Love between two people exists when their YOU COUNT feelings are as strong as their I COUNT feelings."

When we do not let each other know that I COUNT and that YOU COUNT, love flies out the window.

On top of the world

We both know how good it feels when our I COUNT is high. During such times I really feel good about myself. I feel "on top of the world."

I feel alive. I feel capable and "cope-able." I feel hopeful. I can more easily make decisions. I trust people and enjoy their company. I feel warm and loving toward myself.

Let's each try to recall a recent occasion when our individual I COUNT feelings were high.

(We'll tell each other about these experiences in just a moment, when we read the next section.)

"I wouldn't call two 'Gesundheit's in seven years a sincere effort to communicate."

Drawing by Geo. Price; © 1971 The New Yorker Magazine, Inc.

In recalling these experiences, let's ask ourselves such questions as:

What brought on my I COUNT feelings?

Did *I* do something special to raise my spirits? For example, did I treat myself to something out of the ordinary, like calling an old friend long distance? Did something work out well on my job? Did one of my children do something that made me feel proud?

Perhaps *you* did something special for me. You let me know that I was important to you. You complimented me or said nice things to others about me. You phoned me in the middle of the day and invited me out to lunch. You mixed me a nice drink when I came home. Out of the blue, you put your arms around me and gave me a loving hug. We had wonderful sex together.

Maybe you just smiled or touched me warmly. Or perhaps you listened and showed that you understood how I was feeling.

Let's talk about some recent events that made each of us feel I COUNT. It could be something we have shared, or an occurrence that you or I experienced independently of one another.

Let's put the book down and look at each other. I'll talk about a recent experience that made me feel good. Then you can tell me of an event that led you to feel good about yourself.

Let's do this right now before we go on to the next section.

My I COUNT bank

When I feel worthwhile and likeable, I can more easily let you know that you also are a likeable and worthwhile person. In other words, when I feel I COUNT, there is a good chance that I will help you to feel that YOU COUNT also. I can afford to withdraw "reserves" from my I COUNT "bank" and deposit them in yours.

For example, if I were feeling good about myself right now, I would be less likely to turn on you if you happened to be cranky and irritable. I might express sympathy and give you reassurance. I could even go a step further. If I felt that you were miffed at me because of something I had done, I might apologize for my actions and try to make amends.

Now, let's discuss the questions below *one at a time.*

During our discussions we should feel free to express ourselves. But let's try to stick to the main questions and avoid being sidetracked or bogged down in "I'm right—you're wrong" arguments.

When you express your point of view, I should try to say to myself, *"What can I learn from what you are saying?"* rather than, "How can I show you up?" and "How can I prove that you are wrong?"

Both of us will respond to each question. Let's look at each other when we converse. Also, let's remember to return to the program at the end of our discussion and to go on to the next section.

These are very important instructions. Let's reread this section before we go on to the questions in the next section.

1. In general, do I see myself as a worthwhile person?

Before each of us answers this important question, we might ask ourselves:

Was my childhood filled with "You can't," "You're wrong," "You're no good," "You'll never make it," "You'll never live up to our expectations," and "I have no time for you?"

Or was I frequently praised, loved, valued and encouraged to try out new things?

Nowadays, do I tear myself down, blame myself excessively and dwell on my weaknesses and failings? Or do I accept my limitations, learn from my mistakes, and see myself as an OK person, despite my shortcomings?

Do I feel good about myself? Do I feel deep down that I COUNT?

Let's *each* talk about this before going on.

? 2. From what experiences do I get I COUNT feelings these days? Do I achieve self-worth mainly through my job or as a result of other individual accomplishments? Or do I get I COUNT feelings mainly from our relationship?

Again, before reading the next question, let's each express our views on the subject.

? 3. In what ways do I get the feeling of I COUNT from you?

? 4. What are some *positive* things I would like you to do that would give me a greater feeling of I COUNT?

? 5. One divorcee exclaimed, "I put so many eggs into our marriage basket that the bottom of the basket fell out."

Do I have enough separate activities of my own that make me feel good about myself? Or do I put all my I COUNT eggs into the marriage basket and depend mainly on you for my I COUNT?

(Let's remember to express both of our viewpoints before going on to the next question.)

? 6. Am I more understanding and appreciative of you when my I COUNT is high? Am I easier to live with?

? 7. Were we able to discuss these questions without getting into an "I'm right and you're wrong," or "I'm the good guy and you're the bad guy" hassle?

Boosting my I COUNT

I often try to boost my I COUNT feelings by becoming involved in activities and situations in which I feel comfortable and at which I excel. I am also drawn to people and situations where I get praise, respect, or appreciation. On the other hand, I tend to avoid people and activities that threaten my self-esteem.

Below are a few statements by other couples that show the tie-in between my I COUNT feelings and my daily social activities.

Here and throughout the rest of the program, let's take turns reading the parts in the dialogues. We'll read our respective *He* and *She* roles.

She: I can't carry a tune, so I avoid singing. I feel foolish singing out of tune. But I just love acting. You don't have to twist my arm to get me to volunteer for a part in a play. I just eat up applause.

He: I'm no good at finances. That's why I don't handle the bills. I'm fed up with making mistakes. You're a whiz at it, so I'm all for you taking over.

She: I always enjoy talking to our neighbor, Frank. He hangs on to every word I say. You enjoy the tube. You hang on to every word the sports announcer says.

He: If there's one thing I hate, it's cocktail parties. They're so noisy. I usually don't know anyone. I feel like a bump on a log.

She: I'm really into photography. For the first time in my life I'm proud of something I can do on my own.

He: I enjoy biking with my kids. I feel closer to them. I feel more worthwhile as a father.

She: My husband, Ken, thinks my half-time secretarial job is a stupid idea. From a logical point of view he is right. But from a psychological point of view I know I am right. Ken says it's silly of me to work in a noisy, grubby warehouse. He also says it doesn't make any sense, spending almost as much on baby sitters as I make on the job. I know it doesn't add up financially; but the boost I get from being needed and appreciated by the people at the warehouse more than makes up for the low pay.

Do our I COUNTs clash?

Sometimes an activity or an attitude can elevate my I COUNT, but it also may push yours down. A familiar example is that of the person who works excessive hours or is overly absorbed in pursuits that build up her or his ego. Meanwhile, the partner feels left out and unappreciated.

Fred, a successful middle-aged business executive, did a lot of volunteer work that kept him away from home a great deal. He was active on a number of boards and committees, for which he received a great deal of praise and appreciation. This contrasted with his life at home, which he described as "one big, fat I DON'T COUNT as far as I'm concerned."

He complained that his wife did nothing but criticize him. He declared, unhappily, "In my wife's eyes I'm a complete bust as a father and husband. She finds fault with me when I'm gone and tears into me when I'm at home. It's a no-win situation."

Fred's limitations as a family man are quite understandable if you know anything about his upbringing. He had been raised as an unwanted, only child. Both his parents worked and were gone a great deal. They expressed very little interest in him. As a result, Fred was left to his own resources. He grew up like a strong, independent weed. He prided himself on his ability to go it alone, an ability that helped him become a successful businessman.

One does not have to be a psychologist with a Ph.D. degree to predict that Fred would have some difficulties after marriage. As could be expected, he found it hard to live up to the traditional roles of husband and father. Closeness and intimate companionship were not his bag. At home he felt hemmed in and uneasy. He therefore grabbed every opportunity to get away from his home situation. Even when he was at home he really was not there psychologically. He was too busy reading or writing reports.

While Fred felt inadequate as a family man, his wife, Ann, excelled as a mother and housekeeper. Her home and her children were her major sources of I COUNT. But in relation to Fred, she felt ignored, unwanted, and I DON'T COUNT. Even when he was with her, she felt alone.

Fred's social involvements away from home boosted his I COUNT, but lowered Ann's feelings of self-worth.

Ann's home life elevated her I COUNT, but it made Fred feel quite small.

Their I COUNTs clashed.

Here are several other examples in which differing attitudes produce conflicts in I COUNTs.

The first illustration involves a young couple, Jack and Terri. Let's read our respective *He* and *She* roles.

Jack: I like to feel needed (I COUNT). I just love to do things for you. It makes me feel good.

Terri: I feel worthwhile only when I do things on my own (I COUNT). It makes me feel like a helpless child (I DON'T COUNT) whenever you do things for me.

Grace and Scott also have an I COUNT clash. Grace is a "hawk" and Scott is a "dove" when it comes to expressing their feelings.

Again, let's read our respective parts.

Grace: I'm all for letting our emotions hang out. If something's eating inside of me I let it right out. I feel swell (I COUNT) after a good fight or a good cry and then we make up.

Scott: Shouting and arguments are for the birds. They drive me straight up the wall. Whenever you start yelling, I want to crawl into the nearest hole. I just can't stand fighting over every diddling little thing. I always come out the loser (I DON'T COUNT).

1. Do any of these situations ring any bells with us? Does my striving for I COUNT ever clash with yours? Are there any activities that I'm involved in, or attitudes that I express, which boost my I COUNT but lower yours?

Let's talk about some of our own I COUNT clashes before going on to the next question. Let's also try to avoid getting into an "I'm right—you're wrong" or an "I've got to win and you've got to lose" argument while we discuss this important subject.

2. Could we now talk about some activities that boost *both* of our I COUNTs—that make us both feel good?

TIME TO TALK

I DON'T COUNT

When my feeling of self-worth is low, I feel small and unloveable. I lack self-confidence. I feel unimportant, like a no-account, a zero, or a schnook. I don't like myself.

I feel that I DON'T COUNT.

All of us have I DON'T COUNT feelings. We all know how it feels to be snubbed, to be laughed at, or to have a door slammed in our face. When I suffer disappointments, when I can't cope, or when I just plain goof up, I feel momentarily inadequate, depressed, or worthless. My spirits are not lifted when I'm yelled at, ridiculed, or ignored.

If deep down I feel inherently worthwhile and good about myself, I recover from my slump and things look up again. If, however, I do not have these deep-down feelings of self-worth, it's harder to shake off my I DON'T COUNT and bounce back. I'm likely to have such thoughts as:

"What's the use. Nothing I do seems appreciated."
"I feel unwanted and unneeded."
"Whatever I do turns out wrong. I'm jinxed."
"Some people feel like a million dollars. I feel I'm made of Confederate money."
"I feel that if I made a phone call, everybody would hang up on me. Or if someone gave me a dime to phone a friend, I wouldn't know who to call."

Let's try to recall a recent occasion when our I COUNT was low.

Did I feel that you ignored me?
Did I feel that you were rude to me, or that you didn't appreciate what I did for you?
Did I feel that you were more interested in someone else than in me?
Did I feel badly because I could not deal effectively with a problem? Did I make a fool out of myself?

ROTHCO

"When are you going to come out of that protective shell of yours?"

Let's try to remember such specific occasions and tell one another about them. I'll begin now. I'll talk about an I DON'T COUNT experience. Then it will be your turn. Let's try to describe what brought on these I DON'T COUNT experiences, and how they felt.

" TIME TO TALK "

The penthouse and the outhouse

Sometimes my I COUNT feelings waver from moment to moment, or from day to day. Andy and Joyce felt this way.

Andy: I feel like a yo-yo. My elevator goes up and down. One day I'm in the penthouse and the next day I'm in the outhouse.

Joyce: Andy, I feel exactly the same way. Sometimes I look in the mirror and say, "Click, click, you'll do, chick." Another time I say, "Uck, uck, you sure are a cluck."

Have you or I ever felt like a yo-yo? Let's discuss this.

" TIME TO TALK "

As husband and wife, we cannot escape having ups and downs. I DON'T COUNT feelings are inevitable in the best of marriages. The only couple who never had any downs is the story-book prince and princess who lived "happily ever after" in Never-Never Land. And since you and I do not inhabit that fairy tale country it is safe to say that there will be many times when we'll ruffle one another's feathers and we'll feel put down, ignored, and I DON'T COUNT.

Happy marriages are not characterized by the total absence of I DON'T COUNT feelings. Couples who consider themselves happy are those whose I COUNT feelings far outweigh their I DON'T COUNT reactions. By the same token, unhappy couples are those who experience entirely too many I DON'T COUNT feelings.

Now let's discuss the questions below. *Both of us* will answer *each* question before we go on to the next section.

1. Do I ever feel I DON'T COUNT when I feel you aren't listening to me or when I don't get a chance to express my feelings?

2. Do I feel I DON'T COUNT mainly:
When you find fault with me or blame me?
When you ignore me or take me for granted?

3. When I feel I DON'T COUNT in relation to you, do I mainly:
Crawl into a shell, pout, or simmer inside?
Fight back or start picking on you?
Keep busy and try to forget it?
Try to talk it over with you?

4. What do we think is the best thing either one of us could do when we feel ignored or put down by the other?

Would it help if either one of us came right out and said, "I feel ignored" or "I feel put down"?

Couple power

In our discussion during this session, we probably brought out the fact that we derive the major share of our I COUNT feelings these days from our individual achievements, from our work, or from friends or children who like, respect, or appreciate us.

We probably also are painfully aware that we are not getting as much I COUNT from our relationship as we'd wish. I strongly want to read the message, "You are a loveable and worthwhile person" in your eyes. And you probably wish to get the same message from me. But so far we have not sufficiently communicated these sentiments to one another. We have not as yet put all of our *couple power* to use.

By couple power we mean our ability to build up each other's self-worth and to promote each other's personal growth and happiness. We put our couple power to work:

When we nourish each other emotionally.
When we treat one another with compassion and understanding.
When we welcome and encourage the expression of each other's thoughts and feelings.
When we work together to resolve our conflicts and problems.

Couple power is based on I COUNT—YOU COUNT.

In future sessions we intend to tap this power within us.

Here is one last question before we end our first session.

Is there anything we can do today, or in the next few days, that will give both of us a feeling of I COUNT?

Many couples try to break up the routine of their lives in some way so as not to continue to take one another for granted. They decide to go out dining and dancing more often or they arrange for a surprise luncheon date. Other husbands and wives take off on mini-vacations over the weekend. Some couples find satisfaction in working around the house together. Or they experience WE COUNT by turning off the TV set and talking to one another. Going for a long walk or taking a bike ride together are excellent ways of bringing us closer and helping us feel good about ourselves.

We have couple power. Why don't we put it into motion?

Let's take a minute or so to talk about some activity we can do together that will boost both of our I COUNTs. It does not have to be a major production. It could be something small. Let's agree on what we'll do, and then let's go ahead and do it.

Wrapping up

I'm sure this session has been a very meaningful one. We've probably brought up and talked about a number of nitty-gritty issues.

Let's review some of the main points of the first session.

1. **The basic psychological need we share is the need for self-worth, the need to feel that I COUNT.**

2. **When I feel good about myself (I COUNT), I'm more understanding and appreciative of you. I can more easily let you know that you also are a worthwhile and likeable person.**

3. **When I'm down on myself (I DON'T COUNT), I'm more prone to be critical of you. The chances are good that I'll let you know that YOU DON'T COUNT also.**

4. **There often is a clash of I COUNTs between us. I may strive to achieve self-esteem through success at work, or through other outside activities, while you may seek I COUNT mainly through our personal relationship. This is a common cause of friction.**

5. **Our couple power can help us build up each other's self-worth. It can promote our personal growth and happiness. It can be achieved when there is an attitude of I COUNT—YOU COUNT.**

Between sessions

I guess nobody jumps up and down for joy when "homework" is mentioned. But I'm sure we realize that review and practice are necessary and beneficial. Learning to improve our marriage is very much like learning to play a musical instrument or learning to master any other skill. Only through practice can new habits be learned. After a while our new ways of relating will become second nature to us.

The "between session" assignments are fairly simple. After each session we'll be asked to participate in several activities. Below are the two activities for this week.

Activity 1. Each of us should reread the first session. We can do this individually. We should read the material slowly so that we can reflect on the ideas.

Activity 2. After we have read the material we should set aside some time to talk about our feelings about the session and our participation in it.

We might ask ourselves such questions as:

Do we agree or disagree with the material?
Do any of the ideas have a special personal meaning?
What can I do, or what can we do in the next few days to put into practice some of the ideas we've discussed?
How can we boost one another's I COUNT? How else can we put our couple power into operation?

Let's arrange a definite time for our second session meeting.

SESSION TWO

Fight and flight

Let's sit close again and share the book. We'll continue to take turns reading each section aloud. We'll do this throughout the program.

Now that we are comfortably seated, with the book between us, either one of us can start reading the next section.

How not to communicate

In this session we'll get some practice in how *not* to communicate effectively. We'll describe and act out several of the main ingredients that make up the unhappy marriage.

Communication is most effective when, in one way or another, we let each other know that I COUNT and that YOU COUNT. On the other hand, our communication suffers when our messages or actions say, directly or indirectly, "You're no good," "You're not likeable," and "YOU DON'T COUNT."

Let's take turns reading a few juicy YOU DON'T COUNT messages expressed by many couples.

She: You'll never learn. It's no use.

He: You're about the worst driver I've ever seen.

She: You're getting sloppier every day.

He: You're never on time—just like your mother.

She: You never tell the truth. You always exaggerate.

He: As far as I'm concerned, you can go fly a kite.

Such YOU DON'T COUNT remarks make us feel small. They shrink our self-esteem. When a YOU DON'T COUNT message is thrown at us, we usually lob one back in a tit-for-tat fashion. Typical of such YOU DON'T COUNT retorts are:

He: Are you calling me a dope? You're no prize package yourself when it comes to brains.

She: Look who's talking about lousy driving.

He: You call me sloppy one more time, you'll be minus one husband.

She: What do you mean I'm not on time? I'm more on time than you are. And leave my mother out of this.

He: Are you calling me a liar?

She: All I can say to you is "get lost."

Drawing by Geo. Price; © 1964 The New Yorker Magazine, Inc.

Fight or flight

In many ways we behave like animals. When one animal is threatened by another, it usually fights or runs. For the sake of physical survival it defends itself by attacking or by running away.

Although we humans usually do not make it a habit of physically attacking or running away from each other, we do fight or run in a psychological sense. We struggle for psychological survival (I COUNT) by fighting with words, or withdrawing through silence. Instead of relying on tooth, claw, and fleetness of foot, we YOU DON'T COUNT each other. I verbally attack you by blaming or finding fault with you. Then you defend yourself and counterattack by criticizing me. Then I defend myself and return the charge. Then you defend yourself, and so on, until we back away from each other to lick our wounds.

We want love and intimacy. But when we get close we jab each other. Even when we withdraw, the battle goes on—inside our heads. We continue to defend ourselves and bludgeon one another mentally. Our momentary truce is like a time bomb, ticking away until the next blow-up.

This is defensive communication. My defense clashes with your defense. Defensive communication is not nurturing. It drains us.

The fight reaction

We'll use the term *fight reaction* to describe such "I'm the good guy—you're the bad guy" and "I'm right—you're wrong" squabbles. Fight reactions occur when we blame, accuse, or belittle each other to our common disadvantage.

Here is a fight reaction exercise in exchanging YOU DON'T COUNT messages.

We'll have to stand up in the middle of the room, *facing each other*. Let's do this now as I continue to read.

(We stand up.)

For the next few minutes we'll express displeasure with one another's behavior. We'll find fault with each other. Let's say such things as:

"You're always hollering at the kids."
"You never pay any attention to me when we go out."
"You spend money like water."
"You're too fat."
"When will you ever start using underarm deodorant?
"You always turn on the darn vacuum cleaner the moment I sit down to read."

Let's try to say things that reflect our actual criticism of one another. We'll take turns.

Each time I say something critical of you, *you* will take one step backward. Each time I get a slam from you, *I* will step back one step. When each of us has made three YOU DON'T COUNT remarks and has taken three steps back, we'll stop.

During this exercise let's not argue or defend ourselves. Let's just criticize each other and take steps backward.

We should remember to take one step backward after each time we are criticized.

If we understand the instructions, let's go ahead. I'll start now with the first fault-finding remark. Then you'll take a step backward.

(After we've criticized one another and stepped back three times, we'll return to our seats and the book.)

TIME TO TALK

After we've gone through the fight reaction exercise we'll discuss the questions below one at a time. When we talk about these and other questions, let's try not to be bogged down by "I have to prove you wrong" debates. Instead, when you express your feelings, I should listen and ask myself, "What can I learn from your statements?"

1. What were we trying to demonstrate by this excercise? What was the meaning behind our stepping away from one another?

Let's discuss this before going on to the next question.

2. How did we feel when we were criticized? Do we ordinarily accept criticism or do we usually react defensively?

Let's talk about this awhile.

3. Do we ever get into this sort of fight reaction where we pick away at each other in a tit-for-tat fashion? If so, who usually "wins"? Who loses?

4. When you "win" a dispute, do I ever do something to even the score so that I "win" while you lose?

For example, after you "win" an argument, do I ever get back at you by being silent, by making sarcastic remarks, by "forgetting" to do things for you, or by turning my back on you that night in bed?

TIME TO TALK

Holy deadlock

What we were trying to show in the previous exercise was our tendency to *distance* one another with downgrading remarks. YOU DON'T COUNT messages drive a wedge between us.

There's a saying, "When couples fight fire with fire, they end up in ashes."

Marriage counselors have a name for this all-too-familiar vicious circle game, in which couples constantly defend themselves while undercutting their partners. They call it "holy deadlock."

Other names for this affliction are "the pride deadlock," "the blame game," "the chain reaction," "the teeter-totter syndrome," and "the descending spiral staircase."

We will call it the *fight-flight reaction.*

When we're caught up in a fight-flight reaction, we become allergic to one another. We give each other "the oven treatment" or "the refrigerator treatment." We "burn" or "freeze" one another. When I feel I'm being treated badly, I treat you shabbily

"I am remaining calm and objective, you fathead!"

in return. We behave as if we were on a see-saw. I push you down. Then you push me down. Life between us becomes a vendetta.

Fight-flight reactions can be compared to viruses that attack our bodies. A virus first inflames and then weakens healthy tissue. It then leaves it susceptible to future infection. In the same way, fight-flight reactions weaken a healthy marriage. They produce a climate in which any minor disagreement is escalated into a major crisis. What well-functioning couples experience as a common emotional cold becomes a severe case of interpersonal pneumonia. A small brush fire is blown up into a raging inferno.

We could give many illustrations of couples who are locked into a fight-flight vicious circle. One example will suffice.

Janice and Victor went to a marriage counselor for help with their sexual difficulties. They have been married twelve years and have one child. Janice is employed as a lab technician, while Victor sells real estate.

Victor complained that for the past two years, Janice has been completely cold sexually. Janice readily admitted that she had lost all physical feelings for him.

Although the problem presented appeared to be a sexual one, beneath the surface Janice and Victor were in the throes of a classic fight-flight reaction from which Janice's sexual unresponsiveness was but one of many spinoffs.

Let's listen to some of their remarks:

Janice: There's absolutely no doubt about it. I have very little sexual feeling for you. I hate to say it, but I recoil when you touch me in bed. To me, sex has become a nuisance. It's an intrusion. Even though my mind tells me I should have warm feelings for you, my body says, "No."

Victor: It's bad enough when your body says, "No." But your mind is one blank wall also. Whatever I say, you take an opposite point of view.

Janice: You're no "positive thinker" either. You can't find anything right with me. At least I come out with my negative feelings. You turn your back on me and stop talking.

Victor: Why don't we get back to the main subject that brought us here—our sex life?

Janice: You're putting the cart before the horse. The reason I'm not a hot momma in bed has a lot to do with your not talking to me. You turn your back on me, so I suppose I'm doing the same to you.

As I look back at it, it all started when I was pregnant with Tommy. At that time you gave me very little emotional support. You were gone night after night when I needed you most, when I was having a rough time. And even when you were home evenings you acted like a deaf mute. You'd watch TV and never say a word to me. The Green Bay Packers were more urgent and important than a sick wife.

I feel we still really care for each other, but you never show me that you care. I never get the feeling from you that I'm wanted. Can you blame me for not responding to you at night?

Victor: But that's how it all began. When you started denying me sex, it made me feel like two cents. There's nothing I could have done about my working nights. I have to call on customers in the evening. I work damn hard, day and night. It's for all of us, not just for me. That's why we have a nice new home and two cars in the garage. But what's the use of it all when I get no love from you? I'd just as soon be digging ditches. You don't appreciate my efforts and the money I bring in. I got tired of being turned down in bed. That's why I didn't talk to you in the evening.

Janice: If I only felt I could be someone special in your book. If you only talked to me and listened to what I have to say, I'd feel loved. Love doesn't begin in the bedroom. It begins in the kitchen and in the living room and the dining room. How can I love you in one room when I feel like nothing in the other rooms?

I guess my body is saying, "If you don't care for me during the day, my body won't care for you at night. . . ."

The blame game

Whenever we are antagonists in a fight-flight tug of war, we blame one another excessively. Actually, there's nothing wrong in finding fault with some of the things we do. But when I blame you repeatedly, the chances are good that you will react defensively and throw the blame right back to me. I blame you, then you blame me. It's the same as what happens in *Jack and Jill*. Jack falls down and Jill comes tumbling after.

Let's read the parts of "Jack" and "Jill" and act out this "blame game." "Jack" and "Jill," in this instance are real people. They are a middle-aged, middle-income couple who have been married for twenty years. They are top-notch performers at blame gamesmanship.

Jack: I'm fed up with your blaming my drinking for all our marriage problems. First of all, I don't drink that much. Secondly, if I do drink more than I should, you know who is to blame. It was only when you began giving me the cold shoulder in bed that I started in on the martini bit. How do you think I feel, living with a frigid woman?

Jill: Frigid my elbow. It's just the other way around. I enjoyed sex until you started to drink and act like a slob. And then there's that lousy temper of yours, especially when you have a few martinis under your belt. You never made any advances unless you were drinking ahead of time. And I could never be sure you wouldn't be mad five or ten minutes later. You showed no tenderness, no affection. There was no pleasure leading up to it. Just all of a sudden—bang—and then—poof—it's all over. So I reacted by avoiding the whole darn thing. How could I respond when the whole atmosphere, the whole situation, wasn't the least bit pleasurable or satisfying?

Also, I'm angry at you because you indulge in material things that you don't share with me. I feel that the only way is to hold back sex from you. It's my only weapon. I'm not proud of it, but it's my club.

Jack: What do you mean, "material things"?

Jill: The vacations you took, the golfing junkets you go on. It's all your pleasure and your self-indulgence. Buying liquor by the case, buying autos every year.

Jack: The cars were secondhand. They weren't new. I haven't bought a new car in years, and you know it. Let me set you straight on the sex business. You claim that I have a temper. But I blow up and it's over with. I've forgotten it in an hour. You have just as much of a temper. But you don't blow up. You sit on it. You nurture it. You nurse it day in and day out, by the week and by the month. It's that accumulation of bitterness and anger that pours out into your not having sex with me.

The conversation goes on and on, leading further down the spiral staircase. We may as well leave Jack and Jill and continue with the program.

Blaming is a common form of defensiveness. Psychologists call it "projection." We tend to disown our own faults by "projecting" them onto others. Adam disowned his sin by blaming Eve. Eve turned around and blamed the serpent.

There is an old Turkish saying, "When I point a finger at you, I also point three fingers back at myself." In other words, when I blame someone or something, there is a good chance I am covering up some inadequacy in myself.

A close-at-hand example of the projection of blame occurs when couples read the first paragraph of this section of the program. While reading, one of the partners may stumble and mispronounce the word, "psychologist." When this happens, she or he may say, "Darn it. I forgot my reading glasses," or, "Is this word spelled right? It doesn't look right to me." Blaming the spelling or the forgetting of one's eyeglasses is a common device for concealing one's difficulty in reading.

In a similar way, in a more emotional situation, I may blame or belittle you when something really is gnawing away inside me. For example, I may accuse you of being hostile and uncaring, when in reality I may be unwilling to face the fact that I'm angry at you, or that I'm oversensitive to the slightest bit of criticism or lack of attention on your part.

It is much easier to blame you or see the faults in you than to take a good, honest look at myself. Most of us would rather roar like a lion than feel like a lamb. We'd rather say YOU DON'T COUNT than feel I DON'T COUNT.

Excessive blaming, fault-finding, or excuse-making are sure-fire signs that my I COUNT is wobbly.

Below is an insightful statement from a woman who became aware of her fault-finding tendencies. Harriet's remarks may help us understand how blaming can be brought on by some inadequacy in ourselves that we've been hiding.

> You know, Marv, I've always been annoyed when you developed hobbies or when you got enjoyment out of something. I think there's something in me, a big guilt feeling or something else that's behind my attitude. I was never raised to enjoy anything. Enjoyment was always sinful. I took music lessons for thirteen years. Yet not once was there anything mentioned about enjoying it. Any experience was always a lesson, an education, something you did to elevate or improve yourself. It was never fun.
>
> I think this is the reason I blamed you for being self-centered when you got involved in hobbies. When you would suggest we play golf or go to a movie, I would accuse you of neglecting the children. I could always think of a hundred and one things in the house that would have to be done first. When you suggested we get a baby-sitter when we went out, I insisted that you were uncaring about the children and that you were

interested only in your own pleasures. It's a fault in me that I don't know how to change. Instead of looking at the inadequacy in myself, or my guilt feelings, I'd blame you.

Let's discuss these questions one at a time.

1. Do I ever blame you, or take out my anger on you when I'm really angry at myself, or when I've had a bad day?

Can we give any recent examples of this?

2. Would it help if I gave you a *bad-mood warning,* that is, if I told you:

"I'm in a lousy mood right now. I've had a bad day and I feel awfully edgy."

"I've been feeling bitchy all day. I think you'd better give me a wide berth."

"I've been feeling low and worthless of late. I don't know what's causing it. But what I do know is that I act like a crab whenever I feel this way. I certainly would appreciate it if you were tolerant of my crabbiness and not take it personally."

What do we think of this idea?

The flight reaction

When we're in a *flight reaction,* we move away from one another even further than when we're locked into a YOU DON'T COUNT exchange of put-downs and accusations. Instead of thrashing about like two harpooned whales, we escape into our depths of hurt silence. Usually the flight reaction begins with a verbal YOU DON'T COUNT exchange. Then we decide that the battle is too painful. We beat a hasty retreat. But even though we stop talking, within our minds the battle goes on. The hot war becomes a cold war.

Let's look in at a small segment of a flight reaction between two veteran cold warriors, Colleen and Sam.

Let's read our respective parts.

Sam: I've decided that it's an exercise in futility trying to communicate with you. All that happens is I get my head chopped off. Who needs it? So when I come home, I pick up my newspaper, head for the den, and read. This way there are no points of friction.

Colleen: You can say that again about fewer points of friction. To me it means you care more for your newspaper, boob tube, and den than for me. Why should I want to talk with someone who hasn't the faintest interest in me?

When we're locked into a flight reaction, we behave like clams. We hide behind our hard shells and pretend that the other does not exist.

Here is how Wanda and Harry describe their clam-like existence:

Harry: We act like two boxers afraid to fight. Sometimes we circle around each other looking for an opening. But we're really waiting for the bell to ring so that we can retreat to our separate corners.

Wanda: Yes. We avoid each other like two icebergs floating by in the Arctic Ocean. Sometimes we play the game, "Upstairs—Downstairs." I watch TV upstairs while you watch TV downstairs.

At times we may be engulfed in long, strong silences. We simply stop talking to one another. But our silence may be louder than words.

What is our silence saying when we are not talking? Do any of the following statements have a personal meaning?

She: My silence is saying that I'm mad at you. I'm fed up with you. I want to get as far from you as possible. I'm crawling into my own mental territory.

He: My silence means that if I continue to speak out when I'm angry, I'll regret it later. So I'm shutting up right now.

She: Silence on my part means I want to be left alone to cool off awhile. Later I'll come around.

He: You can read my silence to mean that any further discussion is useless. So keep away.

She: My silence is a way of fighting back without having to fight. I'm a silent fighter. Silence gets you mad.

When we're hurt and silent, what is *our* silence saying? Let's talk about this a bit.

Fear—the enemy of communication

Fear usually creates a block to our communication. Below are a few expressions of some of the common fears that produce silence:

She: I'm afraid that what I say may start an argument.

He: I'm afraid that if I speak my piece then you will speak yours. I'm afraid you'll use what I say against me.

She: I was raised to avoid conflicts and disagreements. I'm afraid of getting into a fight.

He: I'm afraid that what I say may offend you.

She: I'm afraid of being a nag—like my mother. If I say what's on my mind I'm afraid I'll feel guilty afterwards.

What fears prevent us from communicating more freely? Let's talk about this.

Escape artists

There are many ways, besides the silent treatment, in which we avoid one another. Here are a few additional flight reactions indulged in by "escape artists."

1. Getting overly involved in some "project," such as constantly tinkering with the car or getting lost in a hobby.
2. Spending excessive hours at work or in social activities.
3. Being glued to the TV set.
4. Entertaining all the time. If we are afraid to be alone with each other, then having company over prevents a confrontation.
5. Escaping into drink or eating too much.

Do we withdraw from each other in any of these ways?

TIME TO TALK

One of the most drastic flight reactions occurs when either of us escapes into the arms of a lover. In the lover's eyes we probably read the messages, "You are a loveable and worthwhile person. YOU COUNT."

Benjamin Franklin once said, "If there is a marriage without love, there will be love without marriage." A different way of putting this is, "If I don't get the feeling of I COUNT from you, I may get it elsewhere."

There's a great deal of sad truth to old Ben's adage.

"My husband is having an affair with another woman. Is there any way I can find out what she sees in him?"

So what else is new?

The most common flight reaction of all is the tendency to take one another for granted. Nothing new happens. We neither grow individually, nor do we help each other grow.

One wife declared, "All we do is get up, go to work, go home, and go to bed—get up, go to work, go home, and go to bed."

There's a story about an unexciting marriage of this sort. Every evening, the husband would ask his bored wife, "So what's new?" She became progressively more annoyed with him for asking this question, since there was never anything new to report. One day she decided to fix his wagon. She embedded a tulip plant in her hair. That evening, when the husband asked, "So what's new?" she pointed to her head.

"Don't you see? I have a tulip growing from my head!"

The husband looked up and then exclaimed, "Oh! And what else is new?"

"You know what's wrong with us? In thirty-seven years we've failed to establish a meaningful dialogue."

When this is our style of existing, we live together, but separately. One husband called it "our brother and sister act." We live parallel lives like two goldfish in adjacent bowls. When we drift along this way, the flames in our marital fireplace go out.

Here is how Dale and Karen describe their stagnant, dead-end relationship:

Karen: We treat each other like a chair or a refrigerator. We go to each other only when we need something.

Dale: Karen, you can say that again. We both seem part of the woodwork.

Karen: It really gets me down. I feel depressed a good deal of the time. I feel I'd be missed only at laundry time and at meal time. Some days I just want to sit in the closet and stay there. We never say anything other than, "Pass the butter," or "What's on TV tonight?" We just don't communicate.

1. Does this "taking each other for granted—so what else is new?" existence apply to us in any way?

Let's talk this over awhile.

2. In what ways can we put "new logs" into the fireplace of our marriage? What can we do to bring more sparkle and excitement into our lives?

Can we learn something new together?

Can we take bridge, golf, or tennis lessons, or learn to sail?

Can we register for evening courses?

Can we join a square-dance group, or learn to play a musical instrument, or take up yoga, or go camping?

Can we go on mini-vacations, even if it's only to a motel just outside of town?

Can we arrange to meet new people?

Can we work on the house together on Saturday morning?

Can we simply turn off the TV set and talk more?

Talking can be one of our greatest pleasures. Couples who share thoughts, feelings and experiences never have to worry about taking one another for granted. Doing new things together is not only fun. It also gives us a lot in common to talk about.

What can *we* do this week that would add some zing to our otherwise dull lives?

Let's talk this over. But in doing so, let's make *positive* suggestions.

Closeness

Let's try a different exercise now. Fighting and running usually lead to distancing. In this exercise, we'll experience greater *closeness*.

Let's sit in our chairs *facing each other*. We'll sit closely, with your knees between mine, as we hold hands. While doing this we'll carry on a conversation for three minutes. A pleasant, enjoyable topic is preferred. We might talk about a happy, joyful experience we've shared.

Let's go ahead.

TIME TO TALK

After we've completed our closeness conversation, let's discuss these questions one at a time.

1. How did we feel while we were talking in this intimate manner?

2. Are we as close in our daily lives as we'd like to be?

3. Let's recall several occasions when we felt particularly close. Let's tell each other about these experiences.

4. Are we *too* close? Do we stifle each other? Sometimes two people wrapped too tightly together make a small package. Do we need a greater separateness? Do we need more privacy at times, or more individual interests apart from each other?

5. What might we say or do that would give us a greater feeling of closeness?

TIME TO TALK

The "What do you hear me saying?" conversation

We're now going to try out a new way of talking. For the time being we'll call it the "What do you hear me saying?" conversation. We'll get a chance to converse in this new way after we've explained how it works, and after we've looked at a few examples.

The conversation starts when I bring up a topic that I feel is important. It can be a complaint that I've been harboring, or it can be any other subject that means a lot to me—our finances, sex, our children, or our personal relationship. I'll talk to you about this problem as freely as I wish. Your job is to *listen carefully without interrupting in any way.*

When I stop, I'll ask you, "Now, what do you hear me saying?" You will then report back to me, in your own words, the gist of my remarks. You'll paraphrase what I've said.

Here is a short example of the procedure. Let's read our respective parts.

Eunice: I'm not sure we should decorate the living room. A vacation is much more important than a new sofa right now.

Now, what do you hear me saying?

Mike: (reporting back) It sounds as if you'd much rather go on a vacation right now than bother with the living room sofa.

After you report back the thrust of my remarks, I can either continue to talk about the subject or you can tell me your thoughts about it. In either case, we must ask each other, "What do you hear me saying?" before the other person continues the conversation.

The basic sequence, then, is:

First I present my views, and then ask you, "What do you hear me saying?" You then report back what I've said.

Then you present your views on the subject, followed by "What do you hear me saying?" I then report back what you've said.

We keep talking in this manner until we've fully expressed ourselves or until we've reached a satisfactory resolution of our problem.

Before we try out this new way of talking, there's one word of clarification. In responding to your "What do you hear me saying?" question, I should try to be like an honest news reporter who is reporting what he or she sees and hears. I *should not* try to editorialize or give interpretations of your statements.

Here is an illustration of what *not* to do. It's an example of editorializing and interpreting rather than reporting back.

It's the same couple—Eunice and Mike.

Mike: I think it would be a wonderful idea if you would go along with me and the kids when we go skiing. It would make us feel like a whole family again. When you stay home we all miss you.

Now, what do you hear me saying?

Eunice: (interpreting) You seem to have an obsession about my going skiing with you. You harp on the "whole family should do things together" theme quite a bit. It sounds as if you are guilty about not spending as much time with the family as you think you should.

A more desirable response would have been:

Eunice: (reporting back) You very much want me to go skiing with you and the kids. You feel it would be good for the family.

We'll now read our respective *He* and *She* parts as we present a bigger slice of a "What do you hear me saying?" conversation. Then we'll have a chance to try it out ourselves.

Nancy and Mark are a young couple, married three years. They both are anxious to improve their relationship.

Mark: (starting the conversation) What I'd like to bring up is what sends us both into our shells. We often start talking about something and then after we say one or two things, we back away from each other. I think we have to find some way of communicating so that we don't draw away from each other, but instead get closer together.

What do you hear me saying?

Nancy: You're saying that through our conversations we go into a shell. You wish we could find some way to get out of this silent trap we get into so we can start talking to each other like two people.

Mark: That's right.

Nancy: (continuing the conversation) The thing that keeps coming back to me is how this got started in the first place. We'll have to find out about that. But the one thing I do know is that I had to bring it all out in the open and tell you that there was something wrong.

Now, what did I say?

Mark: You didn't bring it out in the open. I did.

Nancy: That wasn't what I said. You can defend yourself later. Right now you should report back what I've just told you.

Mark: You're right. What you said was that as I kept drawing into my shell you drifted away from me. You don't know how it all got started but you found some other avenue of satisfying your needs, I guess. That's why you got involved with Ted. . . .

I know your affair had a lot to do with our poor communication. We stopped talking and became silent enemies. Maybe if we fought it out in the open, or at least discussed things more, you wouldn't have gotten hooked up with Ted, damn it.

Now what am I telling you?

The conversation goes on this way. When we follow this style of communication we start listening more. Usually, in a heated discussion, I listen to you with only part of one ear. The rest of me concentrates on defending myself and preparing a "You're wrong and I'm right" retort. However, when you ask me, "What do you hear me saying?" I'm compelled to put myself in your shoes. I listen more carefully. I don't argue as much.

This method of conversing will not only help us to resolve our differences, it also will help us to disagree without being disagreeable.

Let's try out the "What do you hear me saying?" technique. Let's follow the examples on the previous pages by asking *each time,* "What do you hear me saying?" after expressing our views.

We can bring up any subject for discussion. But let's try to make it a real-life problem, something that has been on our minds. Let's remember to ask, "What do you hear me saying?" after each presentation of our thoughts. If you forget, I'll either remind you to say it, or I'll report back what you've said.

Either one of us can start the conversation right now before going on to the next section.

TIME TO TALK

After we've completed our conversation, let's ask each other these questions. We'll discuss them one at a time.

1. Did we ask each other, "What did you hear me saying?"

2. Did we find it difficult or easy to talk in this manner? (We may have difficulty at first in asking, "What do you hear me saying?" It may seem stilted and awkward. However, it will become easier with practice.)

3. Did our discussion deteriorate into an "I'm right—you're wrong" argument, or did we listen more and act less defensively?

TIME TO TALK

The red alert

When we're engaged in a "What do you hear me saying?" conversation, we often bring up touchy, emotional subjects that may upset us. There is a danger that we may be overwhelmed by our hurt and angry feelings, and our conversation may deteriorate into a defensive, fight-flight brawl. In most instances, this danger can be averted if we stick to our "What do you hear me saying?" format by listening to each other and by asking, "What do you hear me saying?"

"I hear you saying you urgently wish someone would come to your aid."

If, however, our conversation gets out of hand, *I should press the red-alert button* and say,

"Let's STOP. There's DANGER AHEAD. I'm gettng too upset over our conversation. We're getting into a fight-flight hassle. I'd like us to *stop* right now. Why don't we hold a 'What do you hear me saying?' conversation about this later, when we've cooled off a bit?"

The *red-alert* is an important emergency measure for nipping our defensive, fight-flight reactions in the bud. When we hold a "What do you hear me saying?" conversation later on, the chances are it'll be a more rewarding one.

It's senseless to try to communicate or resolve a problem when we're out to destroy one another. It's like trying to eat a bowl of soup when it's boiling hot. We simply get burned. We have to wait for the temperature to go down.

Of course, we should not reach for the alert button on every single occasion that we feel angry or whenever there's the slightest amount of emotional flak between us. At times it may be highly desirable to let off steam if it helps clear the air and if it brings us closer together. We definitely should lean on the button, however, whenever we sense a destructive, emotional overkill, an "I'm going to bury you" flavor about our interchange, or when we feel our conversation is going around and around in circles, heading absolutely nowhere but down.

We should feel free to use the red-alert button at any appropriate time throughout the program or during our daily living experiences.

Wrapping up

This is the end of our second session. It has been a fairly long session.

Let's review some of the main points we've covered.

1. **Fight and flight reactions are the two major forms of poor communication.**

2. When we're engaged in a fight reaction, we discount each other with YOU DON'T COUNT messages. When you try to express yourself, I'm not interested in listening or trying to understand you. My main concern is self-defense and retaliation. You also defend yourself and try to put me down. A vicious circle develops. Each of us feels, "I'm right—you're wrong," "I'm the good guy—you're the bad guy" and "You must change." We distance each other.

3. In a flight reaction we retreat from the battle. Each of us feels, "What's the use? If I express myself any further, I'll only get rebuffed. So why continue?" We retreat into a hurt silence or we withdraw into a "So what else is new?" sort of existence.

4. When we blame and accuse each other, there's a good chance that we're covering up some inadequacy in ourselves.

5. One of the main objectives of this program is to help us to cut down on our defensive, fight-flight reactions and to develop an attitude of I COUNT—YOU COUNT.

6. The "What do you hear me saying?" conversation provides excellent practice in I COUNT—YOU COUNT communication. It enables us to listen to and understand one another.

7. We should press the "red-alert button" whenever we sense that our conversation is degenerating into a destructive, fight-flight brawl. We should arrange to hold a "What do you hear me saying?" conversation as soon as we've cooled down a bit.

Between sessions

Did we follow through on the first "between sessions" activities?

This week we'll be asked to participate in the same two activities as last time, plus a third activity involving a "What do you hear me saying?" conversation.

Activity 1. Before we start the third session, each of us should reread the second session.

Activity 2. After our individual readings, we should get together and discuss our reactions to the material. We can ask ourselves such questions as:

What part of the session was most meaningful for me?
Are we too defensive with each other?
How can we best avoid fight or flight reactions?
What can we do to put into practice some of the ideas we've read and discussed?

Activity 3. Let's pick a time in which we can get together and hold another "What do you hear me saying?" conversation.

If we wish, we can use the Activity 2 questions, listed above, as our topic for the conversation. Or we can select any problem that has been on our minds.

Let's try to avoid defensiveness and blaming. Let's also try to stick to the main issues. Our goal is to listen to and try to understand each other. Our goal is *not* to triumph over or demolish each other.

Either one of us can start the conversation. Above all, *let's be sure to ask one another,* "What do you hear me saying?" after each presentation of our views.

If we own a cassette or a regular tape recorder, it would be very helpful, after each session, to tape our "What do you hear me saying?" conversations. We then can play back our conversations and evaluate them.

Whether we use a tape recorder or not, we should ask each other:

How well did we listen to each other? Did I really tune in to what you were saying, or did I concentrate mainly on defending myself and proving you wrong?
Did we focus on the basic issues, or did we get sidetracked?
Did we ask each other, "What do you hear me saying?"
Was it necessary to press the "red-alert" button?
Was it a productive conversation?

SESSION THREE

The I COUNT ladder

Let's draw our chairs together as we start Session Three.

As soon as we are settled comfortably, either one of us can begin by reading the next section aloud. We'll continue to take turns reading each section.

What do we mean by "communication"?

In Session Two we got a pretty good idea of how not to communicate. From here on we will concentrate on how to improve our communication.

What do we actually mean when we use the word "communication" or when we talk about "improving our communication"?

If we were to look up the word "communication" in the dictionary, we'd most likely read such definitions as "an interchange of thoughts and opinions," "a transmission of information," and "a sharing of meaning." These are accurate descriptions of the word. But communication between us, as we'll use the phrase in this program, has a much deeper meaning. When we communicate, we share much more than opinions and information. *We share ourselves.* We open doors to each other. We tell each other what we believe, how we feel, and who we are.

How open and honest are we?

Can I tell you what is really on my mind without fear of starting an argument or being clobbered by you? Will I be ridiculed or laughed at if I admit to mistakes or tell you what worries me, or what I'm scared of? Do I have the courage to speak out about my loneliness, my fears and hopes, as well as my warm feelings for you? Can I let you know that I need more love and understanding, or that, at times, I wish to be left alone? Can I talk to you about our sexual relationship without getting up-tight?

If most of my answers to these questions are "No," then our communication could stand some improvement.

Wouldn't it be wonderful if we could be entirely honest and share each other's thoughts and feelings freely?

This idea probably sounds scary since we are accustomed to holding back and disguising the expression of our emotions and beliefs. We are afraid of hurting or of being hurt. We may fear that really honest communication will backfire and we'll wind up in the I DON'T COUNT doghouse.

Yet, the aim of this program is to encourage a greater openness and expressiveness between us, while cutting down on hurting each other. *Our goal is to maximize expressiveness and to minimize defensiveness.* This is what we mean by "improving our communication." Our relationship will grow if we can honestly share our deeper thoughts and feelings.

In the remaining sessions we will have many opportunities to translate these ideas into concrete behavior.

Getting to know me

Many of my thoughts and feelings differ from yours. Even when we agree, we reveal our differences. We may share similar views on politics, religion, or sex. But the *feelings* that lie beneath my beliefs are uniquely mine. For example, we both may agree in our attitudes toward "open marriage." But we may differ greatly in the *feelings* each of us has on the subject. We do not experience our opinions with the same degree of intensity or conviction.

My thoughts and feelings, together with my actions, are what make me special. They make me a somebody rather than an anybody. My feelings and attitudes are important and deserve to be expressed.

In order to express myself, I must first *tune in* to my thoughts, feelings, and wishes. I must get to know *me* better. The more aware and the more at home I am with what is going on inside me, the more clearly will I be able to communicate.

What are my unique, individual experiences?
They consist mainly of:

1. ***My sense impressions*—what I see, hear, taste, touch, and smell.**
2. ***My thoughts*—what I make out of my sense impressions, the *meaning* I give to what I see and hear and touch.**
3. ***My feelings*—of happiness, sorrow, sadness, fear, guilt, anger, embarrassment, love, joy, or hope.**
4. ***My wants*—my desires, wishes, expectations, preferences, and intentions.**
5. ***My expression*—how I express my thoughts, feelings, and wants.**

My I COUNT ladder

My sensing, my thinking, my feeling, my wishing, and my expressing are the five activities that make me a unique person. These experiences make up my I COUNT ladder—my ladder of self-worth. (I'll read the steps of the ladder from the bottom up, from 1 to 5.)

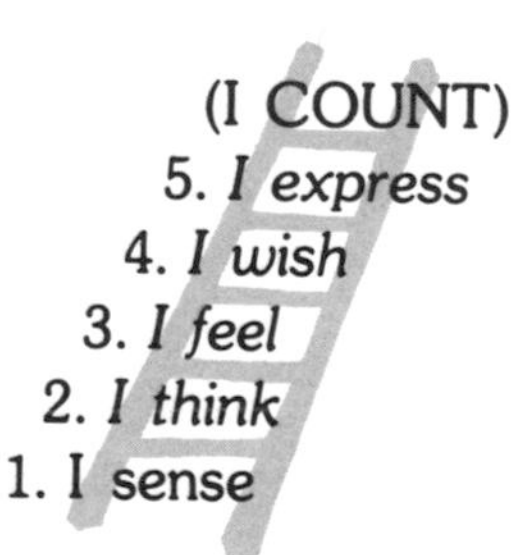

My I COUNT ladder is me. When I climb my I COUNT ladder I tune in and express my thoughts, feelings, and wants. There are many ways of increasing my feelings of self-worth. One of the best is by revealing my I COUNT ladder and by having it respected by you.

My senses

My five senses (sight, sound, touch, smell, and taste) are basic to my experiencing of myself and to my reacting to you.

Here is a simple exercise in using our senses. In this exercise we'll be using our sense of sight and touch.

Let's turn our chairs toward each other. We'll sit facing each other, close together, holding hands, as we did in a previous "closeness" exercise. Let's do this now.

(After this is done I'll continue to read.)

While sitting in this position, let's look at each other *silently* for thirty seconds. Let's observe each other's eyes, nose, hair, and facial expression. At the same time, let's experience how it feels to hold hands.

Let's go ahead now. I'll put the book down as we do this. I'll count to thirty to myself and tell you when the time is up.

After we've done this, let's follow through on the suggestions below, one at a time.

1. Let's describe to each other what we *saw* when we were looking at each other.

2. Let's describe how it felt to *touch* each other and hold hands.

3. How did we feel during this exercise? Did it feel comfortable, strange, awkward, or did it feel enjoyable?

4. Do we look at each other enough? Do we touch each other enough? Let's discuss this.

TIME TO TALK

My thoughts

I'm not simply a creature of sights, sounds, and smells. I do not simply sense. I also try to *make sense*. I give *meaning* to what I see, hear, and touch. My thoughts consist mainly of the meanings I make out of what I sense.

A common problem between us is that you and I may see, hear, and experience the same things but we differ in the *meanings* we give them. Below are a few examples of this. Let's read our respective roles.

She: I see Carol squeezing your arm. I think that she wants to "make it" with you.

He: I feel Carol squeezing my arm. I think that she is trying to hurt me.

She: When you came home this morning I gave you a nice, warm kiss.

He: You didn't kiss me. You were dead tired and you just flopped on me.

She: I see that the bottle is half filled with wine. I think, "Great. We still have half of it left."

He: I see that the bottle is half filled with wine. I think, "Darn it. Half of it's gone already."

Another problem is my tendency to give a favorable meaning to what *I* say or do. But when *you* behave in the same way, I may give it a less favorable meaning.

For example:

She: I can "make quick decisions." *You* are "impulsive."

He: I am "human." *You* are "overemotional."

She: My cutting remark is "clever." *Your* cutting remark is a "cheap dig."

He: I am not afraid "to say what I mean." *You* are "mouthy."

She: My angry outburst is "righteous indignation." *Your* angry outburst is a "temper tantrum."

He: I am the "strong, silent type." *You* are "unresponsive" and "uncommunicative."

The pitcher and the glass

We usually give similar meanings to simple statements and acts. For example, if I were to say that today is Tuesday, or if I asked you to pass the butter, most likely you would agree on the date and you would pass the butter. However, in many ordinary situations, especially emotional ones in which our self-worth is involved, we are less inclined to share identical meanings. The meaning you give to my remarks and actions can be strikingly different from the meaning I intend to convey. My intended message differs from your received message.

What comes out of my pitcher is not always the same as what goes into your glass.

There's a story about a physician who wished to demonstrate to his alcoholic patient how damaging alcohol could be to his insides. The doctor placed a worm in a saucer and then poured alcohol over it. The worm shrivelled up and died. When he was asked what he had learned from this demonstration, the patient replied, "If I ever get worms in my stomach, alcohol is the best thing to take for it."

Such drawing of different conclusions, or the giving of different meanings to what we say or do, occurs, in one way or another, with all of us.

Here, for example, is how two wives gave different meanings to their husbands' snoring.

Virginia: I just can't stand my husband's snoring. It drives me up a wall. I've warned him that if he doesn't stop it, I'm moving into another bedroom.

Pam: Oh, I find my husband's snoring sweet music. When he snores, I know he's in deep sleep and he's getting a good night's rest. Then he's pleasant the next day.

Let's read a few other illustrations of how people give different meanings to each other's remarks and behavior.

Tony, in bed, would reach out toward his wife, Roberta, and ask, "How about some sex, honey?"

Roberta would then push him away and say, "Maybe."

Here is how they both "saw" the situation.

Tony: When you push me away and say, "Maybe," I take it as a sexual rejection. I feel, "What's the use. I guess I don't turn you on."

Roberta: When I say, "Maybe," I'm really hoping that you'll keep caressing me so that I'd get more in the mood. When you quit, I get fed up with you.

Clark and Kristin often misread one another's remarks. Let's read this short example of pitcher and glass confusion.

Clark: Is there any mail today?

Kristin: For God's sake, stop treating me like a dummy. If there was any mail, I'd let you know.

Now the message Clark intended to convey was a simple one. He wanted to know if there was any mail. But Kristin's "glass" heard it as a personal attack.

On another occasion the tables were turned. Kristin greeted Clark warmly and inquired, "How are things? What did you do today?"

Clark replied angrily, "Darn it, Kris, I wish you'd stop snooping into my business."

"I used to think your silences were different!" © *Punch*

Does this ever happen to us?
Do I ever take your statements differently from the way you meant them?
Do I ever take your suggestions "the wrong way"—as criticisms?

Let's talk about this awhile before going on.

TIME TO TALK

More than anything else, *silence* is a producer of different meanings. Silence may be golden at times, but a steady diet of it opens up a whole can of worms in which we constantly misread one another's thoughts and motives. It is like watching a silent movie that has no subtitles. Each of us fills in our own words. Just as a shy person who doesn't say much often is misperceived as being stuck up or aloof, in the same way I can misread your silence.

When I'm silent, do you ever give it a different meaning from the one I intended? For example, when I'm quiet, I may simply be absorbed in my thoughts. But you might think I'm ignoring you or that I'm angry with you.

Does this ever happen with us?

Let's talk about it.

I think it was Carl Sandburg who wrote:

"How can we be pals
When you speak English and I speak English,
And you never understand me and I never understand you?"

The inability to share identical meanings can take a heavy toll in our lives. Misinterpretations can cripple even the best of relationships. Unless we develop some way of checking out each other's meanings our communication can become a comedy of errors—except that the comedy is not very funny.

We have taken a step forward in cutting down on misunderstandings by making use of the "What do you hear me saying?" technique. In later sessions we'll learn additional ways of getting our glasses and pitchers together.

My feelings

I am not only a creature of my senses and thoughts, I am also a feeling person.

We cannot overstress the importance of our feelings. In a close relationship like ours, our emotions influence everything we say or do. Our feelings color and shape how we see and hear each other. They determine what we think and how we behave.

For example, when I feel warm and loving I will see mainly your good traits. Or if I do notice your faults, I play them down or see them in a favorable light. But when I feel hurt or angry with you, I see and hear only your bad points.

We all know the saying, "Love is blind." When we have strong affection for one another, especially during our courtship days, we "see" each other in the best of possible lights.

For example, a young woman, engaged to an immature, irresponsible man, saw these personality traits as boyish charm. Another woman saw her silent, uncommunicative fiance as a deep thinker.

One husband, who was fond of his overweight wife, saw her as pleasingly plump. Another husband declared, "I just love everything about my wife. Others see her as skinny. But I see her as lithe as a gazelle. She could stand on her head and spit bee-bees and it still would be fine with me."

When we are fond of someone, we "see" that person in ways that build up his or her I COUNT.

Hate has sharp eyes

There is an old expression, "Hate has sharp eyes." It is the opposite of "Love is blind." When I'm angry at you, my eyes behave like a lens in a camera operated by a clever cameraman. I can zero in to your faults. I can blot out your virtues.

Here are a few examples of how anger can sharpen our vision in a negative way. Let's read our *He* and *She* parts.

He: When Nancy and I are nice and loving, she admires many things I do. She especially likes my outgoingness, my friendliness with people. But when she's sore at me, she doesn't see me as a sociable, good guy anymore. She sees me as an operator and a manipulator. She calls me hypocritical and deceitful.

She: I used to have nothing but praise for Gordon's strong convictions and his ability to take a strong stand on issues. But ever since I found out about his affair, I see him for what he really is. I've taken my blinders off. Gordon is nothing but a loudmouthed, prejudiced bigot. He's another Archie Bunker.

He: My wife claims that, whenever I'm in a foul mood, nothing she does pleases me. I must admit she's got a point there. She's really a swell person. But if I feel under the weather, or feel mad about something, I'm bound to find something wrong with her. I've criticized the way she runs the house, the way she disciplines the kids and the way she drives. I've even panned her bridge playing, even though she's a much better player than I am.

When I feel ignored, neglected, or upset do I ever start noticing *your* defects? Do I begin to see mainly the "bad" things in you and ignore your good qualities? In other words, do I discount you when my I COUNT is low?

Let's discuss this. We'll try to give some recent examples that show how our moods and I DON'T COUNT feelings affect how we see each other.

"" TIME TO TALK ""

When we lock horns in a fight or flight reaction, our anger and hurt feelings influence how we interpret each other's behavior and how we react. We can both look at the same event, but what I see differs from what you see. My perceptions help to maintain my I COUNT. Often, they lower yours.

Here is an example. Let's listen in to Pete and Gladys.

Pete: Do you know what happened last week? My nervy neighbor, Ralph, was over at our place. He threw his arms around Gladys and kissed her! I just happened to catch them at it.

Gladys: What he's talking about is the New Year's Eve party we had at our house. Ralph came into the kitchen where Pete was standing. Ralph said to him, "Pete, I'm going to kiss your wife. It's close to midnight." And Pete even nodded, "Okay."

Here's another example:

John: My wife is trying to make a mama's boy out of our son. She is always buying him girl's dolls. The other day she even bought him a little mop.

Mary: I'm not "always" buying him girl's dolls. When our boy was three months old, I picked up a neighbor's discarded *boy* doll. It's the only doll he's ever had. He'd pick it up and coo over it. When I mop the floor these days, he wants to help. What's wrong with a boy helping around the house sometimes?

When our feelings change from positive to negative, the ways in which we see each other also change.

For example, a father and his daughter, Donna, were attending the graduation exercises of her husband, Alex. At one point in the ceremonies one of the women graduates was called up to receive her diploma. Donna remarked that this woman was the number one student of her class. Whereupon her father exclaimed, "She sure looks like a cute, sweet gal."

Then Donna told him that this woman was the person Alex had been having an affair with while she and Alex were having marital difficulties. Her father then remarked, "Boy, she sure looks like a creep."

Although seeing is believing, all too often, *believing is seeing.* When our feelings change from negative to positive, we see each other in positive terms.

Feeling, acting, and telling

As children, we were probably reprimanded when we expressed strong feelings. Our parents told us, "Don't raise your voices," or "Children should be seen, not heard." We were supposed to smile and pretend that everything was hunky-dory even though we felt lousy inside. Because of these experiences we are sometimes ashamed of our feelings.

One husband stated, "When I was a kid, I used to run to my mother and hug her around the legs. She would push me away and say, 'You shouldn't touch ladies.' Maybe that's why I feel so guilty whenever I think of touching you."

Were we taught to suppress our feelings when we were children?
Were we permitted to express our anger?
Were open displays of affection encouraged?
Was sex frowned on?

Let's talk over these questions.

It is true that in order to become a civilized person we must curb many of our actions. However, there is a vast difference between having a feeling and acting on it. Like all mortals, I experience selfishness, loneliness, helplessness, inadequacy, jealousy, fear, and anger. At times the thought may flash through my mind that I'd like to throttle you. And I'm sure that at times you would like to beat the tar out of me. These flashes are perfectly normal. It would be wonderful if life were all "bluebirds and pussywillows" and we did not have such negative, unpleasant impulses. But *having* these feelings is part of my being human. *Acting* on them by hitting you is a horse of a different color.

Yet these unpleasant feelings are mine. They are part of my I COUNT ladder. At times I can't avoid being angry with you. When this happens, I have a right to tell you about it if I choose. I could say, "I feel very annoyed when you say that," or "It bothers the heck out of me when I have to keep reminding you to turn off the lights."

Telling, rather than acting out my anger, reminds us of the story of the Hindu guru who was trying to convert a dangerous snake to his philosophy of nonviolence. The snake protested,

"How can I protect myself if I'm not permitted to bite?" Whereupon the guru replied, "You are not supposed to bite. But that doesn't mean that you can't hiss."

Telling you about my feelings is much more desirable than burying them or acting them out in a harmful fashion.

The rhinoceros in the kitchen

We all have embarrassing, painful, or angry feelings. But we often pretend they are not there. We try to tune them out. Unfortunately, sweeping negative feelings under the rug is like having a rhinoceros in the kitchen and pretending it's not there. You may close your eyes to it, but you can be darn sure its presence will cramp your cooking style.

Here is a familiar example of the "rhino who was not there."

Laura: You've been awfully grouchy all evening. Is there anything wrong?

Harvey: There's nothing wrong at all. I'm perfectly fine.

Laura: You chewed the kids and me out. You griped about the newspaper coming late. Are you still angry with me over the argument we had this morning?

Harvey: Can't a guy get some peace and quiet around here? I tell you I'm fine, for cripe's sake.

It's interesting that toward the end of the program he remarked:

> Before, Laura would ask me, "Are you angry with me?" I'd answer, "No, I'm not angry with you." Now when she asks, "Are you angry with me?" I say, "Maybe I am." Who knows, some day I'll say, "Yeah, darn tootin' I'm angry!"

Jack-in-the-box

Strong feelings, like anger, may be suppressed. But they do not vanish easily. In one way or another, suppressed anger pops out like a jack-in-the-box.

Suppose I'm vexed at you for making me go someplace. Instead of voicing my objections, I go along with you without saying a mumbling word. Before we leave, however, I may dawdle and make us late. When we arrive at the place, I may arrange things so that we'll have a bad time. I may make unpleasant remarks about you in front of others. Or I might grumble about what a lousy time I'm having.

Below is a list of some of the more common forms anger takes when we do not talk about it openly.

1. **Belittling you or poking fun at you in public.**
2. **Not listening, tuning you out.**
3. **Monopolizing the conversation, not giving you a chance to express yourself.**
4. **Forgetting what you ask me to do.**
5. ***Never* forgetting what you tell me, remembering hurtful remarks for a long time.**
6. **Dawdling and being late.**
7. **Avoiding you by getting overly involved in some project.**
8. **Turning my back on your sexual advances.**
9. **Developing psychosomatic symptoms—head, back, or stomach aches.**
10. **Becoming tense, tired, sleepy, bored, or depressed.**

Do any of these ways of displacing anger apply to ourselves? Let's discuss each of the ways.

Passing the hot potato

When I'm annoyed about something that has nothing at all to do with you, I may pass my irritations on to you. I hand you my

BERNHARDT ROTHCO

"If you feel like meditating, at least you could meditate out loud!"

emotional hot potato. For example, my supervisor may have bawled me out. Or my car broke down after I just had it repaired. Or the kids were running me ragged all day. Or I may have a splitting headache.

I feel tense and I'm anxious to find an opportunity for releasing my bottled-up feelings. I look for a scapegoat. And guess who is the most likely target for displacing my tensions? You or the children. But I just can't start yelling at you out of the blue. I need some excuse or justification.

What do I do? Most likely I will put into action the most delicate and clever camera in the world—my eyes. Without even being aware of it, I quickly focus on something "wrong." I may see something I do not like. I may notice, for instance, that the evening newspaper lies scattered on the floor, or that the TV is turned on too loud. These, or any other imperfections, become the "border incidents" that touch off my fuse. They give me the green light to unburden my frustrations on you or the kids.

The displacement of tension often occurs when a woman feels tense and cranky just before her menstrual period. Gertrude, a thirty-year-old woman, called this time of the month "my two day wing-dinger." During her "wing-dinger" days little things would bother her that ordinarily would go unnoticed. Invariably, she would find something objectionable about her husband's behavior and zero in on it.

For example, when her husband, Max, walked into the kitchen one day and asked, "What's for dinner?" she snapped back, "Yeah, that's all I'm good for around here—a cook. Wow, did I marry a sexist!"

Do these incidents of displaced tension ever occur with us? Do we pass our emotional hot potatoes to each other?

Let's discuss this a bit.

Bad-mood warnings

A good way to avoid such unnecessary strife is to give one another *bad-mood warnings.*

When the weather is bad, radio and TV stations usually issue bad road condition advisories and announce storm warnings.

Beware of slippery roads and choppy waters!

In marriage, we are very much in need of signals like these to tell us when the psychological weather is bad. Gertrude, for example, could have said, "It's that time of the month again. I'm going to act like a witch, so don't be surprised if I jump down your throat."

Let's read a few additional bad-mood warnings.

He: I have a horrible headache. If I snap at you, it's probably not your fault.

She: I've had a rough day at the office. Something's been bugging me all day. I feel like a gun that wants to go off.

He: I feel like being left alone now. I'm just too riled up.

She: It's getting close to that time of the month. I feel like carrying around a poster that says, "Fragile, handle with care."

It would be wonderful, whenever our inner emotional weather vanes are turning in the breeze, to give out with bad-mood warnings. (Of course, like all good things, bad-mood warnings should not be overdone. They should not be used as an escape from communication.)

It is amazing how *telling you* about my upset state will help relieve my tension. It is also helpful when you encourage me to vent my frustrated feelings and tell you more about what is bothering me. Or you may choose to say or do something that would boost my I COUNT. You can be sure I would appreciate such considerate treatment.

Do we ever give one another bad-mood warnings? What do we think of the idea? Let's talk about it a bit.

Now let's each of us pretend we're in a foul mood. Let's take turns giving one another a bad-mood warning.

TIME TO TALK

Now we'll go through a short exercise in expressing some of our feelings in a direct way. We'll read an exchange of statements. The statements may not be exactly true for us at the moment. However, they are familiar feelings that we often keep locked up inside ourselves. Rather than keeping you in the dark about my feelings, or saying "There's nothing wrong," when I'm really upset, these comments can help you to know what is going on inside me. When I open myself up to you this way, you don't have to second-guess my mood or my behavior.

She: I feel hurt inside when you ignore me.

He: I feel ignored when you take me for granted.

She: I feel like punching you.

He: I'm angry at you.

She: Sometimes I feel helpless and inadequate.

He: At times I feel ridiculous.

She: I feel lousy. If I jump at you for anything you do, it's because I've had such a rotten day at school.

He: I'm sorry I yelled at you. I've been feeling so shook up over my salary cut. I feel as jumpy as a cat.

She: I've been feeling I DON'T COUNT all day. I could use a few positive strokes.

He: My I COUNT is dragging the floor. Why don't the two of us go out for dinner tonight?

She: I feel tender toward you.

He: I love you.

She: I feel sexy when I'm with you.

He: I feel turned on. I'm getting strong vibes from you.

She: I miss you when you are gone.

He: I feel lonely without you.

Body language

We express our feelings mainly through words. But our feelings come out in many nonverbal ways also—through gestures, smiles, frowns, and other bodily movements. We often express our anger or our joy through body language.

Do we bang doors or start the vacuum cleaner when we're annoyed with one another? Do our bodies have a limp, "I'm not here" expression when we're in a flight reaction? Do the ways in which we look at each other or don't look at each other express how we feel?

Usually I'm unaware of most of my nonverbal, bodily ways of expressing myself, but often I'm aware of yours.

I'll tell you some of the ways in which your body communicates messages to me when you are happy or upset. Then you'll let me know some of the ways in which my gestures, facial expressions, or other body movements convey meaning to you.

I'll start.

" TIME TO TALK "

One husband remarked, "When we're upset, you run for the Anacin and I run for the Maalox."

Let's tell each other how the *insides* of our bodies feel when we are hurt, angry, or tense.

" TIME TO TALK "

My wants

The fourth rung in the I COUNT ladder is my *wants*. We all have desires, wishes, needs, and preferences. But many of us are reluctant to come right out and express them. I may be afraid that you would call me selfish if I began a sentence with "I wish. . . " or "I need. . ." or "I would like to. . . ."

Many of us have been taught at home to be more concerned with the wants and needs of others than with our own. In grade school we may have been urged to limit the use of the pronouns

"I" and "me" in our writing and speech. Sunday school teachers may have asked us to memorize the J-O-Y Motto: "Jesus first, Others in between, and Yourself last."

These teachings are all to the good, especially if their goals are to curb excessive self-centeredness. But what we may not have been taught is that there is an important distinction between self-centeredness and self-worth, between selfishness and self-expression. I'm selfish when I make excessive demands or try to coerce or manipulate you into doing my bidding. Real selfishness occurs when I'm overly preoccupied with my needs and my needs alone. I'm selfish when I insist on doing all the talking and when I don't care about your opinions.

You may remember the story about the self-centered actor whose major topic of conversation was himself. At a Hollywood party he spoke all evening about the movies in which he had starred. Finally he stopped talking for about two seconds. He then turned to one of his listeners and said, "I'm tired of talking about myself. Why don't we talk about *you*. Now what do *you* think of my performance in my latest movie?"

I'm not selfish when I replace my slogan of "Big me, little you" with I COUNT—YOU COUNT. "I" is not a dirty word when I use it to express my wants and preferences and respect yours.

Here are a few expressions of my wants. Let's read our parts.

He: I want to go to bed early tonight.

She: I'd just love a back-rub right now.

He: I'm just too darn busy to work on your committee. So I'll have to say "No." I'm sorry.

She: I'd rather go to a show than visit Marge and Sid.

He: I'd like to keep away from you until I can cool off.

She: I can understand why you are disappointed at my not eating the lovely cake you baked, but I'm determined to stick to my diet.

He: I realize that you like this neighborhood and would hate to move away from your friends. But I feel we've outgrown our house. It's entirely too small for our family. I strongly feel we should build a new home.

These statements are not necessarily selfish. They are legitimate expressions of my I COUNT ladder.

The end run

Just as we sometimes suppress our thoughts and feelings, we also hide our wants under a bushel. Or we may express them in a devious, indirect, hide-and-seek manner.

For example, Rebecca wished to visit some friends, the Altmans. Her husband, Will, preferred to stay at home that night and watch several of his favorite TV programs. But instead of coming out with his wish directly ("I'd like to stay home tonight and watch TV"), he used an "end run." He began finding fault with his wife's suggestion.

This was the conversation:

Rebecca: Why don't we visit the Altmans tonight? We haven't been over to see them in a dog's age.

Will: (end run) Don't you ever get fed up with the Altmans? You see so much of Ellen (Altman) at your bridge parties I'd think you'd be sick of them.

Rebecca: Now what's wrong with the Altmans? I never tire of Ellen and I thought you enjoyed their company.

And so the debate about the Altmans rages on. Wouldn't it have been wiser if Will had put his wish on the table and had expressed his desire to stay at home that evening? They might have arranged to visit the Altmans the following evening had Rebecca been made aware of his real preference.

Let's discuss the questions that follow.

1. Does this sort of end run ever occur with us? Do I tend to beat around the bush? Do I often keep my real wishes hidden under a bushel for fear that you might disagree or ridicule me if I expressed them?

Let's discuss this.

2. When I express my wants, are they mainly wishes and preferences? Or are they demands and "You musts?"

Hiding our wishes and intentions from each other can lead to incredible misunderstandings. Here is one example.

Leonard, a university professor, was asked to read a paper at a professional meeting in California. He would have liked to have had his wife, Claudia, accompany him on the trip. But instead of expressing his wish, he kept mum. He assumed she would refuse to go because of the travel expenses. Actually, Claudia would have loved to have gone with him. But since he didn't invite her, she assumed he didn't wish to have her along. Both of their assumptions were dead wrong. When he left without her, she felt awfully hurt and rejected.

On another occasion, Claudia decided to break through their wall of assumptions and second-guessing. The dialogue below illustrates how the direct expression of wishes can open the door to a greater understanding.

Claudia: I wish you would talk to me about your day at the university. I always enjoy hearing about the goings-on.

Leonard: I'd rather not tell you about my problems. I feel it's a burden to you. You don't want to hear them. You have enough worries of your own.

Claudia: That's not true. When you tell me about your worries, I welcome it. I feel you're inviting me into your life. I feel we're partners emotionally.

Leonard: Well, that sure is news to me.

Are we in the dark about each other's wishes?

Let's try out one way of checking out how tuned in we are to each other's desires.

In order to do this, each of us will need a pen or pencil and a small, blank sheet of paper. Let's get this material now.

After we've done this, let's write the letters *A* and *B* on separate lines on each of our sheets, the *A* above the *B*.

I'll now read two sentences which we'll answer independently. Let's move apart so that we don't see each other's answers.

After the letter *A* on our sheets, let's fill in the blank in the following sentence:

A. On the average, *I* would like to have sex with you about _____ times a *month*.

After we've filled in that blank, we'll do the same for sentence *B* below.

B. On the average, *you* would like to have sex with me about _____ times a *month*.

Let's fill this blank before going on.

Now that we've written our answers, let's read them to one another.

Were we accurate in guessing each other's wishes, or were we way off? Did my *A* match your *B*? Did your *A* match my *B*?
Let's talk about this.

Killing each other with kindness

Here's another situation where keeping mum about our wishes can cause confusion. Let's read our respective parts.

Rosemary: What would you like for dinner, dear?

Tony: Anything you wish, dear. Whatever you say is fine with me.

Rosemary: But I'd like to make something that you would especially like.

Tony: You always cook such good meals. Why don't you decide dear?

On the surface Tony appears gallant and considerate. But by not revealing his food preferences, he is placing full responsibility on Rosemary. Since he always passes the buck with his sweet "Anything you say, dear," Rosemary remains chronically in the dark about his food tastes. She also feels strangely guilty whenever he shows dissatisfaction or when she notices his lack of enthusiasm for a particular meal.

Many couples behave like Rosemary and Tony. They often go through an Alphonse and Gaston routine as each defers to the other. They urge each other to decide which movie to go to or which purchase to make. Like the old Alphonse-Gaston comedy act, Rosemary says, "You first." But Tony gallantly responds, "No dear, you first." Or Tony says, "Let's do what you want to do," and Rosemary, like Gaston, replies, "No dear, let's do what you want to do." By being overly "considerate" each dumps the decision-making onto the partner.

This fancy minuet goes on even when the couple reaches the divorce court.

Rosemary: If you want a divorce, dear, I'll go along with it, because you've been so unhappy.

Tony: No dear. If you want a divorce I'll not oppose it. I know you haven't felt happy in our marriage.

Do we ever go through this Alphonse-Gaston routine?

Unlike Rosemary and Tony we'll now try out a short exercise in the direct expression of our wants.

Below is a series of incomplete sentences. They are the beginnings of sentences that we'll complete by expressing our wants. For example, if an incomplete sentence begins with, "I wish you would. . . ," I could complete it by saying, ". . .cut down on your drinking," or by saying something else that expresses my wishes or desires.

Let's read our respective parts and complete the sentences.

She: I wish you would. . . .

He: I would appreciate it if you. . . .

She: What I'd like to continue to do is. . . .

He: What I've always wanted you to do for me is. . . .

She: What *I* would very much like to do for you is. . . .

He: What *I* would very much like to do for you is. . . .

She: I'd like to. . . .

He: I wish I could. . . .

A "What do you hear me saying?" conversation—with feeling

Peggy and Ron are in their early thirties. They describe their marriage as "pretty good, but it could be better." Peggy had been stewing all day over Ron's behavior. At the first free opportunity, Peggy suggested they hold a "What do you hear me saying?" conversation. Ron agreed. Peggy was anxious to air her feelings.

Let's read our respective parts.

Peggy: I'm still fuming at what you said last night.

Ron: What did I say now?

Peggy: It was when you said, in front of everybody, "Peggy, you forgot to dust the piano stool."

"Let me tell you, a lot of women wouldn't put up with your patient, forbearing attitude!" © *Punch*

Ron: What happened was. . .

Peggy: Wait. Let me finish. What got me so blasted angry was that I spent the whole day cleaning the entire house for the company. I vacuumed the living room. I vacuumed the dining room. I scrubbed the kitchen floor. I dusted the philodendron plant. I washed off the piano—the keys and everything. I vacuumed under the piano where the foot pedals are. But I forgot to dust the upper part of the piano stool, darn it. Did you have to be so damn conspicuous about going all the way to the kitchen, getting a towel, and then dusting off the piano stool as if you were performing the most solemn ceremony? I tried my best to ignore it. But I'm still steaming inside over it. I just wish, if I did ninety-nine things right and skipped the one-hundredth, that you would forget the hundredth.

Now, darn it, what am I saying?

Ron: It seems that you are all hot and bothered about what I did about the piano stool after all the cleaning that you did.

Peggy: Yes, and what else did I say?

Ron: What I think you're getting at is that I shouldn't be so picky over one little thing you've done wrong.

Peggy: Yes. Especially in front of company. It's just like the picnic we had last month. I've kept this inside me, so I may as well come out with it now. I worked my rear off getting all the food for forty people. But I left out the salt and pepper. So, in front of all those people, you loudly announce, "You forgot the salt and pepper." I felt like pushing the beans and potato salad into your face. I don't mind your telling me afterwards, but not in front of everybody. Can you see why it upset me so much last night—the salt and pepper and now the piano stool?

Ron: Well, you let your feelings out, so I'll tell you what's on my mind too. I realize I shouldn't have made an issue over the piano stool. But now that you've brought it up, I realize why I said what I did. I was stewing all day. Throughout the day you kept making snide remarks about my wasting a whole day out on the boat. That boat is my hobby, my therapy. Your remarks cut into me. So I guess I gave you the needle about the piano stool.

Now, what do you hear me saying?

Peggy: It wasn't really the piano stool that was bothering you. It was just your way of getting even with me for what I said about you and the boat. The reason I jabbed you on the boat business was because I was in the house working my head off while you weren't helping at all—just fooling around on the boat. Can you realize why I was annoyed with you?

Now, tell me what I'm saying to you.

Ron: You couldn't stand my being in the boat while you were cleaning up the house and getting ready. I wish you had come right out and asked me to help you. . . .

Let's leave Peggy and Ron. They were able to iron out their differences after their suppressed feelings were brought out into the light of day through a "What do you hear me saying?" conversation.

Before finishing this session on the I COUNT ladder, let's hold our own "What do you hear me saying?" conversation. We can bring up any subject or problem. Perhaps we may wish to re-discuss an issue we've brought up during this session.

Let's be sure to *listen* to each other. Let's try to say, "I feel. . ." at the start of a sentence, instead of "You are. . . ."

For example, instead of:

"You are stupid" or "You never listen to me,"

How about:

"I feel annoyed when you say that" or "I feel irritated when you don't listen to me."

Our goal is to *minimize defensiveness and maximize expressiveness*. Let's try to avoid lengthy defensive wrangling. We realize it's very easy to argue defensively. But instead of "I'm right—you're wrong," "I'm the good guy—you're the bad guy," and "I'm going to win and you're going to lose," let's try to adopt an attitude of "I respect my I COUNT ladder and I respect yours." I think, I feel, I wish, and I express; and I respect your thoughts, feelings, and wishes even though we may disagree.

In our discussion let's remember to ask, "What do you hear me saying?" after we've expressed our feelings. Let's avoid editorializing or interpreting when we respond to "What do you hear me saying?" questions. Let's mainly report back the gist of each other's remarks.

Most likely we'll have a successful talk. However, if things get out of hand, let's press the "red-alert button" and arrange for a future conversation after we've cooled down a bit.

I'll start the conversation now.

Wrapping up

After we've completed our "What do you hear me saying?" conversation we will sum up some of the main ideas we've discussed in Session Three.

Here they are.

1. **Communication means sharing with each other. When we communicate well, we open doors to each other's thoughts, feelings, and wishes.**

2. **Our aim in communication is to minimize defensiveness and maximize expressiveness.**

3. **My sensing, my thinking, my feelings, and my wishes, together with my expression of them, make me a unique person. They are my I COUNT ladder.**

4. **There are many ways of building up my self-worth. One of the best ways is by expressing my I COUNT ladder and having it shared and respected by you.**

5. **We often give different meanings to what we say and do. What comes out of my pitcher is not always the same as what goes into your glass. Our differing interpretations are major causes of misunderstanding. The "What do you hear me saying?" technique helps to reduce these misunderstandings.**

6. **Our negative and positive feelings shape how we see and hear one another. When I'm angry, everything you say or do seems wrong. When I feel I COUNT, I notice mainly the good things about you.**

7. **Everyone has embarrassing, humiliating, and angry experiences and feelings. But when we suppress these feelings, they usually pop up again in some devious, undesirable way.**

8. **We should tell each other our negative feelings ("I feel angry" or "I feel upset") rather than act them out in ways that push us apart.**

9. **Bad mood warnings help cut down on unnecessary disagreements and fights.**

Between sessions

Our three activities between sessions are similar to those of last time. We should follow through on these activities if we wish to obtain the maximum benefit from the program.

Activity 1. Each of us should reread the third session.

Activity 2. After our individual readings, let's talk about ideas that are presented. We can ask ourselves such questions as:

What ideas do we agree with?
Which have the greatest personal meaning?
How can we best make use of some of the ideas in order to improve our relationship?

Activity 3. Then let's pick a time to hold another "What do you hear me saying?" conversation. Let's focus on the expression of our feelings. Let's avoid fault-finding and blaming.

After the conversation we should ask the following questions:

How well did we listen to each other?
Have we cut down on our defensiveness and blaming?
Did we ask each other, "What did you hear me saying?"
Was it a productive conversation?
How could we have improved upon our "What do you hear me saying?" conversation?

SESSION FOUR

Tune in and speak out

Let's sit close together again as we continue with the program.

Do we have enough quiet and privacy to go through the session without undue interruptions? If so, let's begin. Either one of us can start reading the material aloud.

Tuning in to my feelings

I have a deep desire to be understood by you. When I'm understood I feel I COUNT. I feel loved.

It would be wonderful if I could open myself up to my deeper feelings and have them shared and understood by you. I would like to reveal my secret fears and inadequacies, my I DON'T COUNT feelings, as well as my hopes, wants, dreams, and triumphs—providing you accept them.

But my strong desire to have you know and understand me is countered by an equally strong wish to protect myself from criticism, ridicule, and rejection. I use my fight-flight defenses to conceal my true feelings. I wear masks. In our daily communication, my mask often talks to your mask.

Part of me, then, is on the side of openness, honesty, being true to myself, and self-disclosure. The other part of me sides with defensiveness, concealment, and "gamesmanship."

We're working to tip the scales in favor of openness. Our communication will improve when we become more aware of our true feelings and when we express them through I COUNT messages.

Tune in and speak out.

Here is a good illustration of bad communication.

Lois sits down to breakfast. Wally, her husband, is seated opposite her, buried in his newspaper. At this moment, if Lois were to become aware of her real feelings, she probably would feel *slighted, ignored, or angry*. But she doesn't tune in and express these feelings. Instead, the following conversation takes place. (Let's read our respective parts.)

Lois: For God's sake! When will you ever learn to stop slurping your coffee? Where were you raised—in a pigpen?

Wally: Oh yeah? In this house I can drink coffee any damn way I please. And since when have you become a model of perfect etiquette?

Lois really felt I DON'T COUNT. But her remarks said, YOU DON'T COUNT. Rather than attacking the issue (her *feelings* of being ignored and her *wish* for him to put the newspaper down), she attacked him.

If she had tuned in to her feelings and had expressed them, she might have said, "*I feel ignored* when you hide behind the newspaper. *I wish* you'd put the paper down and talk to me."

Had she said this, the conversation might have begun something like this:

Lois: I feel ignored when you hide behind the newspaper. *I wish* you'd put the paper down and talk to me.

Wally: I'm not trying to ignore you. I just enjoy reading the paper in the morning.

After this, the conversation probably would have focused on the main issue—her feelings of being ignored versus his wish to read the newspaper.

I COUNT messages

As we indicated in our discussion of the I COUNT ladder, I feel I COUNT when I express my thoughts and feelings and when they are accepted and respected by you.

I use I COUNT messages when I tune in to my I COUNT ladder (my senses, my thoughts, my feelings, and my wishes) and then I express them in a direct way.

In the preceding section, the statements *"I feel ignored* when you hide behind the newspaper" and *"I wish* you'd put the paper down and talk to me" are good examples of I COUNT messages. The wife tuned in to her feelings and wishes and then let her husband know about them.

When we use I COUNT messages, our communication is on the "I" level. We say things "I to I." I COUNT messages often start with such phrases as

"I think. . . ,"
"I feel. . . ," and
"I wish. . . ,"

instead of

"You are. . . ,"
"You should. . . ," and
"You must. . . ."

Of course there are many other ways of expressing my thoughts, feelings, and wishes without beginning with "I feel. . . ," "I think. . . ," or "I wish. . . ."

Below are several other examples of I COUNT messages:

He: I don't like it when you ignore me.

She: It makes me happy when you pay attention to me.

He: I get awfully annoyed when you forget to turn off the lights. *I wish* you would turn them off.

The following is an extremely important I COUNT message whenever we sense the beginning of a fight-flight reaction:

She: I'm getting awfully upset over our conversation. *I'm afraid* we're getting into a fight-flight brawl. *I'd like us* to stop now. Let's hold a "What do you hear me saying?" conversation about this later on.

When I use I COUNT messages, you are less likely to feel belittled and hurt than when I send YOU DON'T COUNT messages. It cuts down on your defensiveness.

Suppose I were to turn to you and say,

"You're so damn lazy. You never take out the trash the way you're supposed to!"

How would you feel? How would you react?

Now, suppose I were to *tune in to my own feelings,* instead of accusing and blaming you. I might then express myself through these I COUNT messages,

"It really bothers me when I have to take the trash out day after day. *I wish* you would take care of it more often."

How would you feel and react now?

Let's discuss the following questions:

If this really happened, would there have been a difference in your reaction to my YOU DON'T COUNT message ("You're so damn lazy. . .") and your reaction to my I COUNT message ("It really bothers me when. . .")?

Which of the two statements would make you less angry and less defensive?

There can be a world of difference in our communication when we send I COUNT instead of YOU DON'T COUNT messages.

ROTHCO

"What kind of rot is that? Four extension phones, a tape recorder, and an intercom—and you say we don't communicate?"

Below is an illustration of how the same problem may be dealt with in two different ways. In the first dialogue, Bev and Carl use YOU DON'T COUNT messages. Like our old friends, Jack and Jill, Bev pushes Carl down, and Carl comes tumbling after.

Bev: When are you going to stop your damn reading? You're the only man I know who reads so much. Why don't you act like other husbands at home. They talk. They don't bury their noses in books.

Carl: Are you calling me a bookworm? I don't give a hoot what other men do. And since when do you know so much about what goes on behind other people's closed doors?

In the second dialogue, Bev decides to tune in to her true feelings. She expresses them through I COUNT messages.

Bev: *I feel awfully left out* when you read so much at home. *I wish* we could talk more.

Carl: I don't object to talking. But what do we talk about? We never have much to say to each other.

Bev: I know we don't have much to talk about. Maybe if we did a few interesting things together we could talk about them.

I COUNT, "I feel" messages

Here are a few statements that reveal I COUNT messages about our feelings:

He: I feel on cloud nine when you praise me.

She: *I'm getting upset* over our conversation. We're getting into a fight-flight hassle. I'd like us to stop talking a bit so I can cool off.

He: My I COUNT is dragging the floor today.

She: It scares me when you drink so much.

We know, of course, that feelings are different from thoughts and opinions. For example, if I were to say, *"I feel that* it's going to rain today," that would not really be an expression of my feelings, even though I used the words, "I feel. . . ." Actually, what I really meant was, *"I think that it will rain."*

"I feel that it's going to rain" and *"I think that* it will rain" are good examples of I COUNT, "I think" messages rather than I COUNT, "I feel" messages. Usually when I start a sentence with "I feel *that*. . . ," I'd be expressing an opinion. But if the word or phrase after "I feel. . ." describes my emotion ("I feel *sad*" or "I feel *annoyed*" or "I feel *good*"), then I'd be expressing a feeling.

"I feel annoyed when you ignore me,"
"I feel happy when you sit down and talk to me," and
"It scares me when you drink so much"

are all illustrations of I COUNT, "I feel" messages.

Now let's pause awhile and take turns expressing three I COUNT, "I feel" messages to each other.

I'll start with the first one. Then we'll alternate.

Now that each of us has expressed three I COUNT, "I feel" messages, we'll carry this idea a step further.

In this next exercise we'll get some practice in replacing YOU DON'T COUNT messages with I COUNT, "I feel" messages.

First, I'll read a YOU DON'T COUNT message. Then, I'll try to put myself in the shoes of the person whose thoughts I'm reading. I'll then express the same thought, this time by using an I COUNT, "I feel" message.

For example, if I were to read the YOU DON'T COUNT message,

"You always say the most ridiculous things,"

I might then replace it with the following I COUNT, "I feel" message,

"*I get annoyed* when you say such things."

Below are a few more YOU DON'T COUNT messages. We'll take turns converting them to I COUNT, "I feel" messages.

We'll read our respective parts.

She: (YOU DON'T COUNT message) When will you ever learn to be on time? You're always late.

She: (I COUNT , "I feel" message) ____________________

He: (YOU DON'T COUNT message) You waste too much time on the phone. Stop being so darn gabby.

He: (I COUNT, "I feel" message) ____________________

She: (YOU DON'T COUNT message) You don't want to spend time with the kids. All you want to do is loaf around and watch TV.

She: (I COUNT, "I feel" message) ____________________

He: (YOU DON'T COUNT message) You clumsy nitwit, you got your dress dirty again.

He: (I COUNT, "I feel" message) ____________________

I COUNT, "I wish" messages

I COUNT messages also can be used to express my wants. They help me express my wishes, desires, and intentions in a direct way that cuts down on misunderstandings.

Here is an example of what we mean:

Sylvia: (I COUNT, "I wish" message) I wish we wouldn't bring up disagreeable topics to talk about after we've gone to bed.

Stan: Gee, that's news to me. I always thought you loved those discussions in the wee hours of the morning.

Sylvia: I don't like them one bit. (I COUNT, "I wish" message) *I'd much rather* talk about personal problems during the day.

Here's another example:

Stan: Whether we go to a movie tonight or stay at home isn't the main issue. (I COUNT, "I wish" message) *What I want to do* is spend more time with you. I rarely get a chance to see you these days.

Sylvia: Why didn't you say so? (I COUNT, "I wish" message) *I'd love* to stay at home and put some records on the player and talk to you. I'm glad you told me how you feel.

There is nothing wrong with my *telling* you my likes, dislikes, wishes, and preferences. But in most instances, I would be lowering the boom on your I COUNT if I insisted or demanded that *you must* unequivocably accept my desires and wishes.

Which of the two statements below would you regard as preferable?

1. "You're getting sloppier every day. You've got to do something about the mess in the living room. If you don't start picking things up pronto, I'm leaving."

or

2. "I don't like it one bit when you drop newspapers on the living room floor and I have to pick them up. (I COUNT, "I wish" message) I wish you'd pick them up and put them in the magazine rack."

Now let's go through the same exercise for I COUNT, "I wish" messages that we did for I COUNT, "I feel" messages.

Each of us will express three I COUNT, "I wish" messages. These messages usually start with such phrases as,

"I wish. . ."

"I would much prefer that. . ."

"I would like to. . ."

"I would appreciate it if you. . . ."

I'll start with the first I COUNT, "I wish" message. Then it'll be your turn.

Below is a series of incomplete sentences. They are the beginnings of I COUNT messages that we'll complete by expressing our true feelings.

For example, if an incomplete sentence starts with "I feel hurt when. . . ," I may complete it by saying, ". . .when you ignore me," or by saying something else that expresses my sentiments.

Let's read our respective parts. Also, let's try to look at one another when we complete each sentence. Above all, let's avoid arguments. This is an exercise in expressing ourselves, not in defending ourselves.

He: What gets me angry is. . .

She: I get annoyed whenever. . .

He: I feel left out when. . .

She: I feel hurt when. . .

He: I feel I COUNT when you. . .

She: I also feel I COUNT when. . .

He: What gives me great satisfaction is. . .

She: It would make me feel very happy if. . .

He: I would really appreciate it if. . .

She: What I've always wanted you to do for me is. . .

He: I've always wanted to tell you that. . .

She: Something I've never told you before is. . .

He: I feel turned on when. . .

She: I feel turned on when. . .

Owning my thoughts and feelings

No one knows my I COUNT ladder better than I. I'm the world's greatest authority on how I feel, what I think, and what I want. When I express *my* thoughts, feelings, or wishes, I'm really on solid ground. Better than anyone else, I know when I feel sad or happy, loving or spiteful, hungry or thirsty, bored or excited, turned off or sexy.

On the other hand, I can only second guess what you're thinking or feeling or wishing at any given moment. You're a much better expert on what's inside your mind and heart.

When I tune in to my thoughts and feelings and express them through I COUNT messages, I take full responsibility for what's on my mind. I speak for myself. I *own* my feelings.

The five steps of my I COUNT ladder (I sense, I think, I feel, I wish, and I express) are my *five freedoms.*

They also are my *five responsibilities.*

Disowning my thoughts and feelings

All too often, instead of owning my feelings, I may *disown* them. Or I might try to own *your* feelings.

Although it may not be the most prudent thing in the world to blurt out any thought or feeling that pops into my head, leaning in the opposite direction is equally harmful. I may treat my feelings like a stepchild or like the black sheep of the family. I refuse to be associated with them. I disown them.

We've already discussed a few common ways of disowning our feelings. They are:

1. **Suppressing our angry feelings;**
2. **Using "end runs" by skating around the direct expression of our wishes;**

3. **Playing the blame game. I disown certain undesirable traits (anger, jealousy, inadequacy) in myself and project some fault onto you.**

Owning your thoughts and feelings

Another way of avoiding the "owning" of feelings occurs when I own or usurp *your* feelings. When I own, or rather "misown" your feelings, I become an authority on your I COUNT ladder. I become your mind reader, your parent, or your conscience. I tell you what you think, feel, or want.

He: You don't want to see that TV program.

She: You're too tired to go skiing.

He: You're silent because you're chicken. You're afraid to communicate.

Here is an example of a husband owning his wife's feelings and wants.

Grace: Frank, I'm going to tell you something that I've been thinking about for years but never told you before. There's nothing I'd enjoy more than going to Florida on our vacation. Just you and I without the kids. I'd just love to relax completely and lie on the beach all week and do absolutely nothing at all.

Frank: (Owning her feelings) You know you don't really want to go to Florida. You don't really want to leave the kids. You'd be worrying all the time about their being sick. And you know you're too active to just sit around on the beach all day.

The sad consequence of owning or usurping our partner's thoughts and feelings is seen in a wife's bitter remarks. After twenty years of marriage, Julia finally mustered the courage to voice her resentment at the manipulation of her wishes by Grant, her "husband knows best" partner. With tears in her eyes she declared:

> Grant, we got off on the wrong foot right after we were married. I must not have gotten to you. Nobody paid any attention to what I was saying. When I quit working for the dentist, my big dream was not to work again. When I told you this, *you said* I really did want to work and that a job would be the best thing in the world for me. *You said* you weren't going to have a lonely bride sitting in the apartment waiting for you to come home each night.
>
> So you got me a job *you said* I'd enjoy—writing copy for the publishing firm. I hated every day of it. I'm not a creative writer. I never have been. Every morning I was out of bed at 6 o'clock. I did it for fifteen years and was sick and tired of it every single day. I would have loved to have been at home doing my own thing.

"Don't tell me what to dream!" ROTHCO

Do we ever own or usurp each other's thoughts and wishes? Do we try to brainwash each other? How often do we say, "You should," or "You must"? Let's discuss these questions.

"TIME TO TALK"

I COUNT messages that say YOU DON'T COUNT

When I speak for myself through I COUNT messages, my main focus is on expressing my thoughts and feelings. What I say, however, involves *you*. Quite obviously a positive I COUNT message ("I like you") is my way of telling you that YOU COUNT, that I care for or respect you. Even when my I COUNT message reveals my irritation ("I get angry when you lie to me"), it is less likely to give you a low I COUNT feeling than would an outright, negative YOU DON'T COUNT message ("You are a liar").

But not all I COUNT messages say YOU COUNT. Some have a decidedly downgrading, YOU DON'T COUNT flavor. For example, take the statement, "I get angry at you when you act like a stupid idiot." One does not need much sensitivity to realize that this remark conveys a strong YOU DON'T COUNT meaning. My pitcher may be pouring out "I get angry," but your glass will pick up, in resounding tones, the YOU DON'T COUNT message "I am angry *at you*" and "you are a stupid idiot."

It is highly desirable (although it isn't always easy) when expressing I COUNT messages to emphasize my own feelings, but at the same time to minimize YOU DON'T COUNT name-calling or attacks on your personality. This is especially true when anger is being expressed.

Anger—the "hurt inside"

All of us experience anger. But have we considered what is behind our anger? My anger doesn't come out of the blue. Something brings it on. Anger usually comes about when I feel hurt or frustrated. Anger really is another word for hurt. When I'm angry I'm hurting.

I have a "hurt inside."

My anger is my *secondary* feeling. My hurt—my worry, my disappointment, my fear, my frustration, and my unrealized expectations—is my *primary* feeling.

I should try to tune in more to such primary feelings and express them.

Let's consider my statement that "I get angry at you when you act like a stupid idiot."

What was the "hurt inside" that produced my anger?

Actually, what brought on my angry outburst was my discovery that you had been speeding on the highway without wearing a safety belt. The "hurt inside" me, that is, my primary feeling, was my worry and fear that you might have an auto accident. In other words, my "hurt inside" was related to *my concern for you.* In contrast, my secondary feeling of anger was aimed at *putting you down.*

An I COUNT "hurt inside" message in this situation could have been, "It scares me to death when you take chances" or "I get terribly worried when you travel at high speeds without wearing your safety belt."

Worry and fear are common "hurts inside" that lie behind our anger. Other important "hurts inside" are embarrassment, disappointment, and frustration.

In most instances, when I am angry, my main "hurt inside" is my feeling of shrinking self-worth. The "hurt inside" is the feeling of I DON'T COUNT whenever I feel belittled, criticized, or ignored.

Here is an illustration of how the I DON'T COUNT feeling can be the real "hurt inside" our anger.

Barb, who worked full-time as a secretary, reported this conversation with her student-husband, Chuck. We'll read our respective parts.

Barb: What a day at the office! I'm dead tired.

Chuck: (YOU DON'T COUNT message) Why should you be tired? All *you* do is sit on your fanny all day and type.

Barb: (YOU DON'T COUNT message) Look who's talking. All *you* do is sit around all day in the library and read.

As we can sense, this conversation has all the earmarks of the beginning of a fight reaction. Chuck sends a YOU DON'T COUNT message. Barb, in anger, replies in kind. (Remember Jack and Jill?)

Let's go through this short dialogue again. This time, however, Barb is going to tune in to, and express her annoyed or angry feelings (in reaction to Chuck's remark), rather than retaliating in a tit-for-tat fashion.

Barb: What a day at the office! I'm dead tired.

Chuck: (YOU DON'T COUNT message) Why should you be tired? All *you* do is sit on your fanny all day and type.

Barb: (I COUNT anger message) I get angry at you when you say such untrue things. I feel like telling you off.

This time, when we role play the same dialogue, Barb will tune in to, and express, the "hurt inside" feelings behind her anger.

Barb: What a day at the office! I'm dead tired.

Chuck: (YOU DON'T COUNT message) Why should you be tired? All *you* do is sit on your fanny all day and type.

Barb: (I COUNT "hurt inside" message) I feel awfully hurt inside when you say that. I work hard all day and I feel you don't appreciate what I do.

I COUNT messages that express my "hurt inside" often are preferable to those that express my anger. When I reveal my "hurt inside" feelings you will be less prone to attack me. Instead, you may find yourself expressing surprise at my feelings.

"Gee, I didn't know you felt that way," or, "I'm sorry I upset you. I didn't know it bothered you that much."

When you criticize or find fault with me, it is desirable for me to respond more often with an I COUNT "hurt inside" message. Instead of retaliating in kind ("When I'm hurt, I hurt back"), I should try to tune in to my hurt feelings and then come out with them in a direct way.

At first, it may be difficult to respond with "hurt inside" statements. We are so accustomed, when hurt or angry, to either fight, flight, or defend. However, with practice, it will become easier to reveal our hurt feelings.

I COUNT "hurt inside" messages usually begin with such phrases as,

"It hurts me when. . ."
"I get frustrated when. . ."
"I feel small when. . ."
"I feel discouraged when. . ."
"It makes me feel I DON'T COUNT when. . . ."

Let's take turns expressing several I COUNT "hurt inside" messages to each other. If we wish, we can begin with the phrase, "I feel hurt when. . ." or "I feel I DON'T COUNT when. . . ."

I'll start.

TIME TO TALK

Now, let's carry this a step further. I will make a remark that will be critical of you. You will then respond with an I COUNT "hurt inside" message.

For example, suppose I were to say, "When will you ever learn to drive right? You keep making wrong turns."

You might then respond with the I COUNT "hurt inside" message, "I really feel humiliated when you criticize my driving."

I'll now start with a YOU DON'T COUNT, fault-finding remark. You will respond to it with an "I feel hurt inside" statement. Then you'll criticize me and I'll respond with an "I feel hurt inside" type of answer.

Let's remember to cut down on defensiveness in our responses. Our intention in this exercise is to use I COUNT "hurt inside" messages, and not to win arguments.

Let's go ahead now before reading the next section.

TIME TO TALK

The first basic communication rule

We can sum up what we've discussed so far in this session by stating our first basic communication rule:

I'll tune in to my own feelings. Then I'll express them through I COUNT messages: "I think. . ."; "I feel. . ."; "I wish. . . ."

Of course we don't have to go around expressing "I feel. . ." and "I wish. . ." sentiments all the time. Our goal, however, is to use I COUNT messages more frequently.

Is honesty the best policy?

We've been urged to be more open and honest with each other.

But is honesty always the best policy? Wouldn't it be too shocking or hurtful if I dropped all inhibitions and told you the "whole truth and nothing but the truth?"

For example, suppose we were to come out swinging with these choice, "right between the eyes" remarks?

He: You didn't get married until you were thirty. That's because no one else would have you.

She: You sure are a lousy lover.

He: By all odds, you were the least attractive woman at the dance.

She: You're an absolute idiot when it comes to art appreciation.

What do you think of this kind of "honesty?"

These tactless and brutal YOU DON'T COUNT slams can hardly be called honest or truthful. This species of "truth" can be a deadly weapon between us. Pointing to your personal and physical deficiencies is like shining a flashlight right in your face. Your eyes will shut automatically. You'll react immediately with anger and defensiveness.

Such "honesty" can more accurately be described as vindictive forms of fight-flight behavior. At best they reveal poor judgment. Most likely these vicious forms of "honesty" allow me to use you as a punching bag or as a dumping ground for my frustrations. They are deeply destructive of our self-worth and can leave lifelong scars.

Some people get an "A" in honesty but an "F" in tact.

Honesty in expressing our feelings is most desirable in a context of I COUNT—YOU COUNT. Honesty is highly recommended when I tune in to my own feelings and use sincere

I COUNT messages instead of malicious YOU DON'T COUNT digs. Instead of telling you unpleasant things about *yourself,* I should tell you about *myself.* In playing the game of "To Tell the Truth," I should let the real me stand up.

Which of these statements are the more honest ones?

He: (YOU DON'T COUNT message) You were the least attractive woman at the dance,

or

(I COUNT message) I was very angry at you during the dance. I felt ignored by you. Right now I feel like saying something nasty to you.

She: (YOU DON'T COUNT message) You sure are a lousy lover,

or

(I COUNT message) I didn't enjoy sex with you last night. I felt frustrated, unloved, and unfulfilled.

Are there occasions when it's best not to bring up certain touchy, "hot potato" subjects for discussion? Should we consider the *time* and *place* and the *moods* we're in when we bring up problems for honest discussion?

The daily powwow

Do we ever find the time to talk things over in an open and honest way? Do we ever sit down during the day or in the evening and have a powwow?

Our days and nights are filled with schedules. Our meals, our working hours, our appointments follow a set ritual. But so few of us bother to schedule a few minutes of the day *entirely for ourselves.*

The Marriage Encounter movement, sponsored by the Catholic Church, urges couples to commit themselves to daily "ten-and-ten" discussions. It's called the Daily Dialogue Encounter. Each partner writes his or her feelings on a given topic in a ten-minute letter. The letters are exchanged and then used as a launching point for a ten-minute dialogue. The daily "ten-and-ten" enables couples to keep in touch and share intimate feelings.

What do we think of the "ten-and-ten" idea? Would we care to give it a try? Or how would we feel about holding a daily powwow in which we could talk about what's on our minds? The powwow can take place during or after a meal, in bed, or while we are out for a walk.

Let's take a minute off and talk about these ideas. Are they worth trying out?

TIME TO TALK

A "What do you hear me saying?" conversation—I COUNT messages

Glenn and Ann, a young student couple, were participating in this program. Earlier in the day they had had an unpleasant fight-flight interchange. Several hours later, Glenn suggested that they hold a "What do you hear me saying?" conversation on how they were progressing with the program. Ann agreed. They decided to express themselves through I COUNT messages as much as possible.

The beginnings of several of the I COUNT messages are italicized.

Glenn: *I think I'm trying* to work at this communication program harder than you are. I'm trying to say what I mean. I'm taking more risks. I'm going out more on a limb. *I feel annoyed* that you aren't doing likewise.

Ann: You're saying that you're trying more than I am to speak out more, but you're not getting much satisfaction from me. It sounds as if you're really teed off about it.

Glenn: Exactly! *I do feel teed off. I'd feel much happier* if you'd work harder at it. *I wish* you'd stick your neck out more and tell me what's on your mind. Take a chance. The worst that can happen is that I'll say something nasty back. But the chances are I won't, unless you clam up as you did this morning.

Now, how do you read me?

Ann: It's the same as what you've been saying before. You want me to stick my neck out and say what's on my mind. You're also saying that you'd be very pleased by it if I did. I think you're right. But when I get uptight, I can't think along these lines. I get too defensive. *I would like to be able* to control myself better, but I feel my efforts aren't enough, and *it upsets me.*

What am I saying to you?

Glen: That you are afraid of me.

Ann: Now, that's not what I'm saying. What I'm saying is that when I get upset, I can't apply what the program suggests. *I just get too darn mad. I feel hurt inside.* One reason I feel hurt and angry is because I don't think you appreciate all the things I do for you. *I really get the feeling of I DON'T COUNT* when you ignore my efforts.

Glenn: You're saying that you're trying. You want to apply what the book is telling us, but you get mad. Your feelings get in the way. Maybe you should just try to express your feelings. If you get mad, then just tell me that. Why don't you say, *"I get so damn mad. I'm boiling inside."* You can even scream it at me.

Ann: I'm afraid that if I really tell you how I feel you'll always hold it against me. This morning, for example, rather than blasting you, I decided to quit talking. *I was too hurt inside* to say something constructive.

Glenn: What you're saying is that you get too mad to say something reasonable, so you shut up. But what I'm trying to tell you is, when you get to that boiling point, why don't you say out loud, *"I'm angry now. I'm darn angry.* I can't talk straight. Let's talk about it tomorrow." And tomorrow you can bring it up again.

Now, what do you hear me saying?

Ann: You're suggesting that if I'm too angry to talk rationally, I should come right out and say so. Then I should talk about it some other time. I should say, "I'm too mad to talk now. Let's quit for now."

"Want to talk about it, Martha?" ROTHCO

Let's go ahead now with our own "What do you hear me saying?" conversation. We can talk on any subject we wish. Let's use I COUNT messages as much as possible, particularly I COUNT "hurt inside" messages.

As we recall, I COUNT messages often begin with "I feel. . . ," "I think. . . ," and "I wish. . . ." I COUNT "hurt inside" messages frequently start with "I feel hurt when. . . ."

Above all, let's remember to ask, "What do you hear me saying?"

I'll start the conversation.

Wrapping up

Our "What do you hear me saying?" conversation brings us to the end of our fourth session. Here is a summary of the main points we've covered.

1. ***Tune in and speak out.*** **Our communication improves tremendously when we become aware of our thoughts, feelings, and wishes, and when we express them.**

2. **I COUNT messages are those statements that reveal how I think, how I feel, and what I desire. I COUNT messages usually start with such phrases as "I think. . . ," "I feel. . . ," "I wish. . . ," or "I would like to. . . ," instead of "You are. . . ," and "You must. . . ."**

3. **I "own" and take responsibility for my thoughts, feelings, and wishes when I use I COUNT, "I think," "I feel," and "I wish" messages.**

4. **Anger is another word for hurt. When I'm angry, I have a "hurt inside." My main "hurt inside" that leads to my anger is my feeling of I DON'T COUNT. Tuning in and expressing my "hurt inside" primary feelings produces a less defensive atmosphere between us.**

5. **Honesty is the best policy when it's expressed in a context of I COUNT—YOU COUNT.**

6. **The first basic communication rule is, "I'll tune in to my thoughts, feelings, and wishes and then I'll express them through I COUNT messages."**

Between sessions

How are we getting along with our "between sessions" assignments? Have we been trying out our "What do you hear me saying?" conversations?

This coming week, before we start the next session, let's participate in these three activities:

Activity 1. Each of us should reread the fourth session.

Activity 2. Then, let's discuss our reactions to the ideas presented in the session.

Activity 3. After this, let's hold another "What do you hear me saying?" conversation on any subject that is of interest to us. Let's make it a point to express ourselves, as much as possible, through I COUNT messages.

Again, after the conversation, let's ask ourselves such questions as:

How well are we listening to one another?
Did we ask, "What do you hear me saying?"
Did we make use of I COUNT messages, including "hurt inside" statements?
Are we cutting down on "I'm right—you're wrong" and "I win—you lose" defensiveness?
Was it a productive conversation?

Between sessions, let's also make more use of "I think. . . ," "I feel. . . ," and "I wish. . ." sentences. Let's keep in mind the first basic communication rule. Before speaking, we'll pause a moment and try to tune in to our feelings. Then we'll express our feelings through I COUNT messages.

Let's be sure to work out a time for our next session.

SESSION FIVE

YOU COUNT

How are we doing?

We're now half way through the program. Before we start this session let's pause a moment and take stock.

How are we doing?

Is our couple power working for us?

To evaluate our progress each of us will need a pen or pencil and a blank sheet of paper.

Let's get this material now.

Now let's write the numbers 1 through 10 in a vertical column on each of our sheets. Do this before going on.

I'm going to read a series of statements which describe how we've been getting along and how we've been feeling about each other *during the past week*. Our responses will help us evaluate our progress.

After I read each statement, we'll write the word **yes** or **no** next to the corresponding numbers on our sheets. We'll answer the statements independently of each other.

Here are the statements:

1. **We've been feeling pretty good about each other.**
2. **We've been tense and unpleasant.**
3. **We've been too busy to share much.**
4. **We've tended to ignore each other.**
5. **We've been talking more.**
6. **Our relationship has been closer and warmer.**
7. **We've had satisfying experiences together.**
8. **Our communication has improved.**

Let's write down our answers to the next two questions.

9. **If there have been positive changes between us since we started the program, what have they been?**
10. **What do we think we can do in the immediate future to improve the situation? What specific steps can we take?**

After we've written our answers, let's compare each of our responses and discuss them.

Let's do this before going on to the next section.

Simple gifts

We'll now focus on the second half of the I COUNT—YOU COUNT method of communication—on YOU COUNT.

Did I ever wake up in the morning, look over at you, and say to myself, "I'm going to do something to make you happy today"? And then I went ahead and did it.

Most of us get swept up in the routines of living and we forget to do the simple things that would please each other.

Here are a few expressions of appreciation for these "simple gifts" that spell YOU COUNT.

She: I felt you were thinking of me when you phoned and let me know you'd be a little late for supper. It was considerate of you.

He: I feel great when I get a hug from you.

She: I was really on cloud nine when you sent those flowers. And it wasn't even my birthday! I felt it was *worthday*.

He: It was Thanksgiving morning. For some reason I felt down and blue. When I said to you, "My I COUNT is low," you took me in your arms and said, "You're special. You have a lot of YOU COUNT in my book." It gave me a fantastic lift.

In marriage, the greatest gift of love is to let you know that YOU COUNT.

There are any number of ways of informing you that you are special, that you are a worthwhile and loveable person. When I listen to you attentively, and when I encourage you to reveal your thoughts and feelings, when I smile at you, when I put my arms around you in an affectionate and supportive way, or when I praise you, I signal to you that I care for you and that YOU COUNT.

In a way, I also let you know that YOU COUNT whenever I express myself through I COUNT messages. When I tune in to myself and then reveal my feelings to you, especially my feelings of hurt and vulnerability, I help you also to tune in and accept your own feelings.

When I reveal my humanness, it helps you to reveal your humanness.

I also convey YOU COUNT whenever I give you a *bad-mood warning*. Instead of cutting you down or finding fault with you when I'm in a foul mood, my emotional distress signal tells you that *the problem is inside of me*. It's only fair to let you know this. After all, if I'm feeling lousy, why should I take it out on you?

My storm warnings also open up opportunities for you to convey YOU COUNT to me. When you become aware of my upset state, you may respond by giving me some extra attention or by doing something else that would especially please me. Or if I prefer to be left alone, you might give me a wide berth.

One YOU COUNT deserves another.

A basic guide to any good relationship is: *"Whatever else we neglect, we should try never to neglect each other's feelings of self-worth."*

We all can use a good pat on the ego.

A good slogan to adopt is:

A YOU COUNT a day keeps the marriage counselor away.

The YOU COUNT ladder

Below is a diagram of my YOU COUNT ladder. It's my ladder of care and concern for you. When I step up the ladder, I let you know that YOU COUNT.

I'll read the steps of the ladder from the bottom up, from 1 to 5. We'll discuss each of the steps during this and the next session.

(YOU COUNT)
5. *I change myself*
4. *I accept your being different from me*
3. *I express an understanding of your feelings*
2. *I tune in to your I COUNT ladder*
1. *I give you positive strokes*

Positive strokes

It is hardly necessary to remind us that sharing our positive feelings for each other is a wonderful way of building a loving relationship. Genuine praise and expressions of love and appreciation are essential to our feelings of self-worth.

Mark Twain once said, "I can live for two whole months on one good compliment."

When we say or do things that reveal our appreciation and affection we give *positive strokes.* This phrase was introduced by Eric Berne, the famous psychiatrist who wrote *Games People Play.* Positive strokes also are called "warm fuzzies." Negative strokes (YOU DON'T COUNT messages) are "cold pricklies."

Positive strokes warm the human spirit. They nourish us and help us to flower and grow. Just as a sapling requires daily sunlight, water, and fresh air, in the same way we need daily expressions of appreciation, understanding, and support in order for our relationship to grow.

Positive strokes are better than vitamins—and they're free.

Negative strokes are like an icy wind. They whittle away at our self-confidence and stifle our personal development.

"You haven't griped about anything all morning. Can I interpret this as a positive stroke?"

Positive strokes usually are verbal. Here are a few examples:

He: I sure appreciate all the time and effort you've put into making the party a success.

She: You have a plus that most men don't have. You are very imaginative. Your mind is alive. You think of many new and different things.

He: You were wonderful tonight. Everything you said and did made me glow inside.

She: You turn me on.

He: You too.

The following remarks are *not* examples of positive strokes:

She: I'd like to thank you for being sober last night. It's a welcome change from your usual beastly behavior.

He: That was a lovely dress you bought. It also had a lovely price tag on it.

Do we tell each other the good things we feel about one another often enough?

Let's talk about this awhile.

TIME TO TALK

Now let's take turns expressing two positive feelings we have for each other. Let's be sure they are positive strokes, without adding any "buts," "maybe's," or negative digs.

I'll start. After I give two positive strokes it'll be your turn.

(If we wish we can start our sentence with, "You make me feel good when. . . .")

TIME TO TALK

Now let's take turns completing these statements:

She: One of your most endearing qualities is. . .

He: One of your most endearing qualities is. . .

She: What I admire in you is. . .

He: What I admire in you is. . .

She: I really appreciate it when you. . .

He: I really appreciate it when you. . .

She: What I miss the most when you are not with me is. . .

He: What I miss the most when you are not with me is. . .

She: One of the things you've done recently for me that I especially liked was. . .

He: One of the things you've done recently for me that I especially liked was. . . .

Keeping in touch

Many of us sadly neglect one important way of expressing positive feelings. Outside of bed we may rarely touch each other.

Deep down, we probably are no different from dogs, cats, monkeys, and other animals who enjoy being petted and stroked. We know that babies require a good deal of stroking and hugging. But as we get older, the need to touch and be touched often gets programmed out of us. We are taught to feel ashamed and embarrassed when we reach out to hug or touch people. When we accidently touch or bump into somebody, we are expected to say "I'm sorry."

How many times have we been told, "Don't touch. It's not nice"?

One of the things we've learned from the sensitivity-encounter movement is that adults do have strong needs for bodily contact. It is amazing how quickly we tap our yearnings to touch and be touched, to hold and be held, to hug and be caressed, when we are given permission to shed our outer armor of aloofness and control, and when we are encouraged to reach out to each other.

Many couples complain of the absence of touching in their daily lives. For example, many wives would love to be stroked, hugged, and have their backs rubbed. Yet they are afraid to ask their husbands to touch them for fear that "he'll just drag me off to bed." These couples haven't learned that "keeping in touch" by petting, holding hands, and hugging, need not always lead to sexual relations.

Are we a couple of "untouchables"?

Do we touch each other much these days?

Would we like to touch each other more?

How?

Let's discuss this a little while before going on to the next section.

TIME TO TALK

Now let's put the book down and stand up. We'll take turns giving one another a positive stroke by touching, stroking, or hugging each other. I'll begin.

(After we tear away from each other, we'll go on with the program.)

Tuning in to your I COUNT ladder

When I tune in to your thoughts and feelings I let you know that your experiences matter to me. Even a simple "How are you feeling today?" or "You seem upset over something; is there anything the matter?" reveals my concern or interest in you. I encourage you to share your thoughts with me.

Let's discuss these questions one at a time.

1. In our daily living, do I encourage or discourage the expression of your feelings?

2. Are there many occasions when I don't know how you think about important matters?

Can I recall any occasions when I was in the dark about how you felt, especially about important issues?

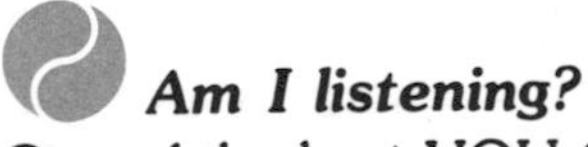

Am I listening?

One of the best YOU COUNT responses I can make is to *listen attentively* to you. People in personal counseling often are exhilarated by the experience of being listened to by a person who does not condemn them for what they say.

Many men and women go to bars or beauty parlors, not to drink or get their hair done, but out of a desperate need to have someone listen to them. There probably would be a sharp decline in the profession of marriage counseling if couples spent more time at home listening to one another.

Attentive listening is very different from *defensive listening.* When I listen defensively I tune in only to the chinks in your armor or to what I perceive are attacks on my personality and criticisms of my behavior. I listen to you like an opposing courtroom attorney, ready to use your statements as a rope with which to hang you.

In defensive listening I tune in only to what I want to hear and tune out what I don't wish to hear. I'm busy formulating counterarguments. My mouth goes into motion before my ears hear the play.

Attentive listening means paying attention to you. If I'm reading a newspaper or watching TV or shoving clothes into the washing machine while you're talking, it's unlikely that I'll hear you fully. Very likely you'll feel that the newspaper, the TV program, or the washing machine counts more than you do.

Attentive listening means taking the time to listen. If I don't have the time or if I can't give you my undivided attention, I could say something like:

"I'm sorry, but I just can't listen to you right now. I have too many things on my mind to listen carefully to you. Could this wait until later?"

In the same vein, Steve, a clothing store salesman, said to his wife when he returned home,

> Judy, I know you want to talk to me as soon as I get into the house. I know you've been stuck at home with the kids all day and you're dying to have an adult to talk to. But I've had a rough day myself and I've been talking all day long. Right now I could use a decompression chamber. I need some rest and quiet. Could it wait awhile? Why don't we talk after dinner? I'm sure I'd be a much better listener then.

In attentive listening I should look at you. My facial expression should let you know that I'm tuned in to you. My comments can also indicate that I'm listening. For example, I might say, "I've been listening to you carefully. I agree with some of your points of view, but I disagree with some of your suggestions for changing my behavior."

Let's discuss these questions one at a time.

? 1. Do I usually listen attentively to you, or do I often turn off my hearing aid?

When you're talking, does my mind often wander?

? 2. Do I often zero in to the weaknesses and flaws in your statements and ignore your main message?

? 3. Do I start talking and answering back before you've finished what you have to say?

" TIME TO TALK "

Let's try out an exercise in attentive listening.

I would like you to talk for *one minute* on any subject you wish. I will listen quietly to what you say. I'll try to absorb the main points of your statements without answering back or arguing.

After we've done this, I'll talk for one minute on any subject while you listen to me in the same way.

Why don't you start first while I listen?

YOU COUNT messages

My attentive listening is the first step in tuning in to your thoughts and feelings and in letting you know that YOU COUNT. A more active, and a highly recommended way of tuning in to you, is through the expression of YOU COUNT messages.

YOU COUNT messages are my way of telling you that *I understand you.*

Each of us craves to be understood. When I feel understood, I feel deeply worthwhile. One of the great sources of strength in religion stems from the feeling that a higher power is listening and understands.

A YOU COUNT message is a statement on my part that says,
"I know how you feel"
"I can put myself in your shoes"
"I'm tuning in to you."

A YOU COUNT message reveals my awareness of your feelings and my understanding of your point of view. It encourages you to speak further on the subject. It helps draw you out rather than put a lid on your thoughts.

A YOU COUNT message usually is said in a sympathetic way even though I may not fully agree with you.

Here are a few examples of YOU COUNT message responses:

She: I'm fed up with everybody making a mess in the living room. Everybody dirties up the place and nobody bothers to pick anything up.

He: (YOU COUNT message) I can understand why you're so upset. It sure is a mess here.

or

He: (YOU COUNT message) I can really see why you're yelling at us. We really should give you a hand.

She: I don't like it when you've got your nose buried in your newspaper when I talk to you about the problems our children are having.

He: (YOU COUNT message) I'm sorry. *I can see why you're annoyed with me.*

He: Can't we get any peace and quiet around here? The TV is on, the phonograph is blaring, and you're yakking on the phone.

She: (YOU COUNT message) I know how you feel. But I'm afraid with the children in the house there's going to be noise.

We'll now try an exercise in sending YOU COUNT messages. We'll take turns reading a number of statements. After you read a statement I'll respond to it with a YOU COUNT message.

I'll then read a statement and you will respond with a YOU COUNT message.

As an aid in expressing YOU COUNT messages we can start our sentences with such phrases as:

"I realize that you. . . ."
"I can see that you. . . ."
"I can understand why you. . . ."
"I really can see why you feel that way. . . ."

Now let's go ahead and respond to each other's statements with YOU COUNT messages.

She: Why don't you ever remember my birthday or our anniversary? You never seem to be aware of any special occasions in our lives.

He: (YOU COUNT message) ______________________

He: What a day! The car wouldn't start. Sales were lousy. My back aches. And now you tell me the washer is on the fritz.

She: (YOU COUNT message) ______________________

She: I'm really getting fed up with my job. It's all just a waste of time. I'm getting nowhere. I wish I could get some other job where I feel I'm accomplishing something.

He: (YOU COUNT message) ______________________

He: Every time I come home, your clothes are all over the place. You're getting messier every day.

She: (YOU COUNT message) ______________________

One key point should be raised here.

We should avoid being phony in our use of YOU COUNT messages. There undoubtedly will be many times when I'll find it hard to express a genuine YOU COUNT message. I may not really understand your viewpoint, or see things the way you do. In such instances, it would be insincere to use such opening phrases as, "I really understand how you feel. . . ."

When I don't see eye to eye with you, I could still make use of a form of YOU COUNT message. I might start with such opening phrases as:

"I don't quite see it your way. . . ."

"I'd like to see it your way, but. . . ."

"I'd like you to help me understand it from your point of view. . . ."

"Could you explain it once again. . . ?"

Suppose you were to say "I'm tired of running away from bill collectors. From here on in, I'm going to be in charge of the budget."

I might respond by stating, "I don't quite see it your way. I thought I had done a good job with the bills. But apparently you don't think so. What is obvious is that you're very upset about the bills."

Although I didn't see it your way, at least I was able to let you know that I was aware of your upset state.

One way in which I do not convey YOU COUNT is by declaring "It's your problem" whenever you bring up an issue or complaint. In many instances the issues you raise may be predominantly your problem and responsibility. But it is also *my concern*. The very least

"All right, I've listened to your side of the argument. Now I'm waiting for a translation!"

I could do is to express this concern either by listening to you or by using YOU COUNT messages. Saying "It's your problem" without expressing my concern is a YOU DON'T COUNT cop-out on my part.

The second basic communication rule

As we recall, our first basic communication rule was:

I'll tune in to my own feelings. Then I'll express them through I COUNT messages ("I think. . ." "I feel. . ." "I wish. . .").

We are now ready for our second basic communication rule:

I'll tune in to your thoughts and feelings. Then I'll express YOU COUNT messages ("I can understand why you. . ." "I know how you feel. . .").

What do you think?

An additional way to express YOU COUNT is through "What do you think?" questions. A "What do you think?" question is my way of asking you where you are at in your thoughts and feelings. It encourages you to share your thoughts with me. Typical "What do you think?" questions are:

"What do *you* think?"
"A penny for your thoughts."
"What do *you* have in mind?"
"How do *you* feel about it?"

In daily conversation, these questions sound like this:

He: What are your thoughts about selling the car?

She: Something seems to be bothering you. Can you tell me what it is?

He: I don't think Jimmy should use the car tonight. What do you think?

She: Let's stay home tonight. How do you feel about it?

Let's now take turns saying things to each other that include "What do you think?" questions. We'll also respond to each other's questions.

Let's read the example below before we try it out ourselves.

She: My mother is planning to visit us next month. *How do you feel about it?*

He: Well, I'm not exactly enthusiastic about it, but I guess she's pretty lonely and would enjoy visiting us for a little while.

First I'll express an opinion on any subject. Then I'll ask you, "What do you think?" After you respond to my question, it will be your turn to express an opinion, followed by a "What do you think?" question. Then I will tell you my thoughts about the matter.

I'll start.

"Do you mean. . ?"

One important way of letting you know that YOU COUNT is by asking you to clarify the meaning behind your remarks.

In an earlier session we discussed the different meanings we give to one another's thoughts, feelings, and actions. What flows from your pitcher is not necessarily the same as what ends up in my glass. This leads to considerable misunderstanding and confusion.

Let's read this example:

She: Last night I heard you grunting and swearing in the bedroom. I felt you were swearing at me. When you dropped your shoes on the floor I felt as if the shoes had fallen on my head.

He: It had nothing to do with you. I was swearing because I couldn't find my glasses.

Our statements as well as our silences are like psychological inkblots. They are often vague or unclear. We can read all sorts of things into them that may or may not exist. Even such innocent remarks as "What's for dinner?" or "How are you feeling?" when strained through my mind, can take on a different meaning from the one you intended.

He: What's for dinner?

She: What's for dinner? What's for dinner? That's all I hear around here. That's all I'm good for around here—a cook and housekeeper.

One good way of avoiding misunderstandings is to ask each other "Do you mean. . . ?" questions. Here's an example:

She: I wish you would observe the traffic signs.

He: Do you mean I'm driving too fast?

She: Yes, that's exactly what I mean.

or

She: No. I'm trying to get you to avoid making U turns. We can't afford any more traffic tickets.

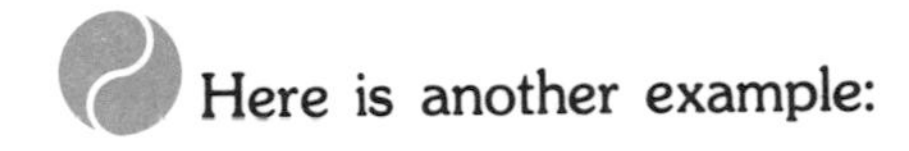

Here is another example:

He: When will dinner be ready?

She: Do you mean you're annoyed with me for not having the meal prepared by now?

He: Well, come to think of it, I am a bit miffed at your coming home late and not having dinner ready by now. Is there anything I can do to help?

"Do you mean. . . ?" questions help to clarify our statements and feelings. They help us share meanings in a more accurate and more productive way.

Let's take turns saying things to each other. After my statement, you will respond with a "Do you mean. . . ?" question. If your meaning is the same as mine, I'll say, "Yes." If your meaning differs from mine, I'll answer, "No," and then I'll clarify my meaning.

Here is an example:

She: I'll be home late tonight, so don't wait up for me.

He: Do you mean you don't want to speak to me when you get back?

She: No. I'll probably get in quite late after visiting my mother. What I mean is, I'd like to catch up on my sleep and go right to bed when I get home. We can discuss mother's problems sometime tomorrow.

Now, I'll say something to you. After I do, you will ask me a "Do you mean. . . ?" question. I will then respond to your question by letting you know whether you've picked up the main meaning of my remark.

I'll start. If I wish I can begin my statement with the phrase, "I would like you to. . . ."

TIME TO TALK

Now, I, your partner, will do the same. I'll say something to you, beginning with the phrase, "I would like you to. . . ." Then you will ask me a "Do you mean. . ?" question. I will then let you know whether you've grasped my meaning.

I'll go ahead now.

What do you hear me saying?

We are already familiar with the "What do you hear me saying?" technique. It's an important YOU COUNT skill.

Responding to "What do you hear me saying?" reminds us of that American Indian saying that we see in souvenir stores:

"Never judge a person until you've walked in his moccasins for one day."

When you ask me "What do you hear me saying?" it gives me a chance to "walk in your moccasins" and to experience your thoughts *as you see them.* I step into your frame of reference. My response is my way of saying, loud and clear, "I'm listening to you. Your ideas and feelings count."

When I'm able to see things from your point of view it can have a number of possible effects:

1. **It can help me to understand you better.**
2. **It will make me less defensive.**
3. **It may lead to a change in my point of view.**
4. **It may help us to achieve a compromise. Or it may result in some other satisfactory resolution of our problem.**

A "What do you hear me saying?" conversation—YOU COUNT messages

Here is an illustration of a "What do you hear me saying?" conversation where YOU COUNT messages were used.

Sally and Ernest, the speakers, have three children between the ages of six and twelve. (Let's read our parts.)

Sally: I'd like to talk to you about the way we're disciplining our children. Is that OK with you?

Ernest: Sure—what do you have in mind?

Sally: I find it disturbing when you don't give me your active support in disciplining the kids. Whenever I tell them to do things, they turn to you and expect you to shut me up. I find it very annoying. Even when you raise your voice to them, they know that I'm pushing you on them. They know that I'm the one who pressures you into doing it. I wish we were more of a team and you backed me up more.

Now, what am I saying to you?

Ernest: I really can see that this is very upsetting to you. I agree that we should talk it over. You're saying that you do all the disciplining while I try to shut you up. You want me to support you in some way. I'd like to be of help to you, but I don't see it your way. I don't see the point in both of us yelling at them at the same time, especially in the middle of a meal. Also, there are many times when you want to discipline them when I don't think it's warranted. Furthermore, I'm not the sort of guy who yells.

Sally: But you yell at me!

Ernest: Wait a minute. (YOU COUNT message) *I know that you want to give your views,* but I haven't said "What do you hear me saying?" yet. I don't feel that I yell at you. I know I should be more supportive of you, but I really don't know what you want me to do.

Now, what do you hear me saying to you?

Sally: (YOU COUNT message) You seem genuinely interested in wanting to help out, but you don't know how. Let me give you a good example of how you can support me. It happened last night. You turned to Pat during dinner, and in a firm voice you said, "That's right. Now you do what your mother says." This was right at the dinner table. You didn't say, "Let's discuss it later." You didn't shush me up. You let the kids know you were with me. I appreciated your support. I felt very close to you. I felt, "Gee, we are partners," even though we didn't say a thing to each other. To me, that's what a partnership is. We can sense what needs to be done without the other person begging for it or resorting to criticism to get attention. If I make a horrible mistake, tell me later, not in front of the kids.

Now, how are you reading me?

Sally and Ernest have made a good start in resolving their disagreement by listening to and understanding each other. Why don't we leave them now and go ahead and hold our own "What do you hear me saying?" conversation. Let's try to use YOU COUNT messages as we discuss any topic of our choosing. YOU COUNT messages are especially appropriate when we respond to each other's "What do you hear me saying?" questions.

Either one of us can start now.

Wrapping up

Let's review some of the ideas presented in Session Five.

There are many different ways of expressing YOU COUNT:

1. **By giving positive strokes—by expressing positive, appreciative feelings for each other.**

2. **By encouraging each other to express ourselves. This includes the expression of unpleasant feelings.**

3. By listening attentively to each other.

4. By expressing YOU COUNT messages—statements that indicate that I understand you or that I can put myself in your shoes.

5. By asking "What do you think?" and "Do you mean. . . ?" questions.

6. By conducting "What do you hear me saying?" conversations.

7. The second basic communication rule is:
I'll tune in to your feelings. Then I'll express YOU COUNT messages.

8. Along with this rule, a good slogan to follow is: "A YOU COUNT a day keeps the marriage counselor away."

Between sessions

Let's follow through on the three basic activities during this coming week.

Activity 1. Let's reread the fifth session.

Activity 2. After our individual readings, let's discuss the ideas and how to make use of them in our daily lives.

Activity 3. Then let's arrange to have another "What do you hear me saying?" conversation. Let's try to make use of YOU COUNT messages, especially when responding to one another's "What do you hear me saying?" questions.

After the conversation, let's ask ourselves such questions as:

Is it becoming easier to hold a "What do you hear me saying?" conversation?
Did we use YOU COUNT messages?
Was the conversation brought to a satisfactory resolution?

Here are several additional questions to consider between sessions:

Have we thought of holding daily powwows or daily "ten-and-ten" dialogues?
Are we making a conscious effort to use I COUNT and YOU COUNT messages?
Are we giving one another bad-mood warnings?
Are my remarks and actions boosting your I COUNT these days? Do they make you feel better about yourself?

SESSION SIX
Changing me—changing you

It's that time again. Let's draw our chairs together and get comfortably seated as we explore our ability to accept or change one another.

Either one of us can start reading this next session.

Goodbye diet

The two of us probably are alike in many ways. We also have many distinct differences.

Differences are not necessarily damaging to our relationship. Life would have very little spice if we saw things the same way and if we reacted to everything as if we were identical sheets rolling off a copy machine. It would be awfully boring if we agreed on everything. A writer once said, "When two people always agree, one of them is unnecessary."

As they say in France, *"Vive la difference."*

We frequently choose partners because of our differences. A vibrant, outspoken woman may be drawn to a quiet, "deep" man. Or a strong, aggressive man may find a meek, retiring woman very much to his liking. If these differences mesh, then the partners get along well. "The rocks in his head fit the holes in hers." All too often, though, we are dismayed by our differences—traits which we were unaware of until we began to live together.

Let's take the example of the "vibrant" and "outspoken" woman who was attracted to the "quiet," "deep" man. This description fits Ruth Ann and Norman to a tee. During their courting days, Norman found Ruth Ann's "dynamic," "alive" qualities highly appealing. Ruth Ann, in turn, said she always disliked “loud, obnoxious men who are always talking about themselves.” She, therefore, cherished Norman’s “kindliness,” “softness,” and “understanding nature.”

After marriage, however, they discovered the other side of the coin. It didn’t take too long before Norman, the dove, was taken aback by his wife’s hawklike behavior. He couldn’t tolerate her “nagging” and her “abrasiveness.” He summed up his frustrations by declaring, “Living with Ruth Ann is like living with one’s nose close to a floodlight. The light is wonderful, but the heat is devastating.”

On the other hand, Ruth Ann resented the way Norman “shriveled up” and withdrew every time they had a disagreement. She called him “my Caspar Milquetoast.”

Before marriage we usually put our best feet forward. Unless we’ve shared many intimate experiences we mainly reveal our *public selves*. After we say “I do,” our *private selves* step forward, warts and all.

Drawing by Geo. Price; © 1970 The New Yorker Magazine, Inc.

*“You **knew** when you married me that I couldn’t shimmy like my sister Kate.”*

A magazine cartoon illustrates this point. It shows a newly married couple driving away from the church ceremony. The bride has a demonic smile on her face as she proclaims, "Goodbye, diet. Hello, pepperoni pizza!"

Someone has said that the honeymoon ends when the bride burns the biscuits and the husband snores. Married life really begins when we start acting like our true selves and start revealing our differences and shortcomings to one another.

Jack Sprat and wife

We are all different. Like squash, we come in all shapes and sizes. All marriages are "mixed" in the sense that couples invariably differ in major as well as minor ways. Even the best matched couples don't see eye to eye on many issues.

As far as we are concerned, we probably are similar to Jack Sprat and wife. You may prefer the lean meat while I go for the fatty parts. I may be a "night person" while you may be a "day person." You may bounce out of bed at sunrise all "bright-eyed and bushy-tailed," while I may drag myself around like a sleepwalking zombie all morning but come to life in the afternoon. I may like classical music while you may like folk songs and bluegrass music.

I may insist on opening the bedroom windows wide at night, while you can't stand it when the temperature goes below 75 degrees. I may want to go out a lot while you are more of a stay-at-home type. I may express my anger freely, while you may sit on your hostility and stew for a long time. I may have a "take-it-or-leave-it" attitude toward sex, while you can't get sex off your mind and are ready to jump into bed at a moment's notice.

Let's discuss these questions one at a time.

1. Were we drawn to each other because of our differences or because we were alike in many ways?

2. What new traits did we discover in each other *after* marriage?

“ TIME TO TALK ”

Let's talk about our differences. In discussing the questions below, let's make it a point to avoid arguments. Let's listen and try to learn from one another. We are trying to explore our differences. We are not interested in debating whether my personality is better or worse than yours.

Let's talk about each question before going on.

1. What are some of the main ways in which we differ?

2. Who is more of a communication hawk and who is more of a dove? Does one of us tend to spout off while the other insists on peace, quiet, and harmony?

3. Who is more the "teflon" type and who is more the "blotter" type? Who shakes off hurts and forgets them easily? Who soaks in hurts like a blotter does and stews over them for a long time?

4. Who yearns for greater privacy and distance? Who wishes for greater togetherness and closeness?

5. A perfectionist has been defined as "a person who takes great pains and then inflicts them on others."

Who is more perfectionistic and who is more easygoing?
Who is more easily dissatisfied and insists on changes?
Who is more content with the status quo?

6. Who is moodier and more changeable from day to day and who is more consistent in daily behavior?

7. Who is the greater spender and who is more of a financial conservative?

8. Do our differences bring us closer and give greater spice to our marriage? Or do our differences keep us apart?

TIME TO TALK

A chip off the old block, or, the apple never falls far from the tree

One of the main reasons for our differences in outlook and behavior is that we've been raised in different families. The eighteen years or so of basic training that I've had in my family upbringing varies considerably from yours. Our individual I COUNT ladders have been very much shaped by these differences in our personal backgrounds.

If I were raised in a rough-and-tumble home, where my parents fought a great deal, there's a good chance that I also will be volatile and expressive. If my parents spent money freely and didn't worry about saving for the future, there's a strong

likelihood that I'll have the same easygoing "chicken today and feathers tomorrow" attitude toward money.

But suppose your parents were quiet, reserved, and never raised their voices. Suppose they also were conservative about spending money. The chances are good that you will take on these traits. As a result, you'll probably be irritated with my "noisy" ways. You'll also be annoyed at my "cavalier" and "irresponsible" spending habits.

If my mother, for example, was a fastidious housekeeper, who was never done cleaning, I'll probably expect you to be neat and orderly also. If you are not as tidy, you can be sure I'll let you know about it.

It often works the other way around. If members of my family behaved in ways that I couldn't tolerate, then there's a good chance I will not tolerate similar behavior on your part.

For example, if my parents argued and fought a lot, I may have developed an intense distaste for arguments and disagreements. As a result, I may be "allergic" to you or anyone else who is loud or assertive. I might overreact every time you raise your voice. As one husband stated, "My mother was always chewing out my Dad. He just stood there and took it on the chin. In my marriage I just won't tolerate any gaff from my wife. I'll close my ears to it."

Or, suppose I were raised by a "wall-to-wall" mother who did everything for me. Suppose I resented her efforts because I sensed it undercut my self-reliance. There's a strong probability that I would wince whenever you tried to do something for me.

We'll now have an opportunity to tune in to our early upbringing and relate it to our present behavior.

Below are two sentences that have blanks in them. After we read several examples of how other couples filled in the blanks, we'll do the same ourselves.

Whenever you ________, I feel ________.
It reminds me of my ________.

Here are a few examples of how other couples filled in these sentences:

She: Whenever you don't help me with the dishes *I feel* indignant. *It reminds me of my* brother Gary. He was never expected to help around the house.

He: Whenever you are not on time *I feel* very irritated. *It reminds me of my* father. He was always late. That's why I get so riled up even when you are a minute late.

She: Whenever you hold me close *I feel* wonderful. *It reminds me of my* Uncle Jim. Whenever he visited he'd play with me, lift me up, and hug me. I loved my uncle.

He: Whenever you hold me close *I feel hemmed in like a bird in a cage. It reminds me* of my possessive mother. She was always watching over me and telling me what to do.

Let's do the same. Each of us will express ourselves by filling in the blanks:

Whenever you ______, I feel ______.
It reminds me of my ______.

One husband said to his wife, "My parents never paid much attention to me. That's why I'm so oversensitive when you don't talk to me."

Are there any experiences in our childhood that lead us to be oversensitive about each other's behavior?

Let's discuss this for a while.

Do we think it would be wise to tune in to our sensitivities and tell each other about them?

For example, I might say, "I feel awfully sensitive about your reading a newspaper during dinner. When I was a youngster, our family would always talk to each other around the dinner table. That's why I can't tolerate your reading at that time."

How do we feel about this kind of tuning in and speaking out?

Accepting each other's differences

Are we familiar with the prayer,

"God grant me the serenity to accept the things I cannot change, the courage to change the things I can, and the wisdom to know the difference."

In marriage, as well as in all other aspects of life, there is a time for accepting and a time for changing.

The greatest YOU COUNT attitude I can show is to accept you as you are. At times I may express irritation with you. But my overall acceptance of you, as a person, with your faults, is one of the greatest gifts of love I can give you.

It's wonderful to be able to give each other room in which to be different. Fellini, the famous film director, once said, "Accept me as I am. Only then will we discover each other."

Accepting you as you are is not easy. Acceptance means that I recognize you as an imperfect, fallible, human being, just like me. Being mortal, you have many failings. Most likely you'll never fit my bill perfectly.

This accepting attitude was reflected in a remark, made half in jest, by a woman whose husband was a Greek-American. She stated, "I thought I was marrying a Greek god. But he turned out to be a god-damned Greek." She then added, "I finally discovered that he was a real human being, not a god."

Accepting you as you are also means having an open mind to your ways of doing things differently from me.

You may prefer, for example, to go on a prearranged, "package" group tour of Europe. You don't want to bother with hotel arrangements, looking for restaurants, tipping problems, etc. On the other hand, I would rather have us rent a car and travel about by ourselves.

You may feel that the dishes should be left to drain and dry naturally after washing. In contrast, I'm a strong believer in drying them with a dish towel.

Both of our positions, in each example, have their advantages and disadvantages. Yet I may refuse to consider any plan other than my own. Only my way is acceptable. I close my eyes to alternatives. I refuse to compromise.

There is a story about a psychologist who performed the following experiment. While a hungry chimpanzee was watching, he placed some lettuce under a box. The chimp was then led out of the room. During his absence the lettuce was removed and replaced with a banana. When the chimp was ushered into the room again, he went straight for the box, expecting to eat the lettuce. But, to his chagrin, he saw, instead, the banana. That was not what he had expected at all! He became so upset over the change that he picked up the banana, threw it to the ground, and then stomped on it.

He must have been a pretty neurotic chimpanzee. His *rigid expectations* prevented him from fulfilling his needs.

Many couples have similar rigid expectations. Central to their attitudes is the phrase, *"You must."*

"*You must* behave the way I want you to."
"Because your ways are different from mine, *you must* be wrong."
"Even though you may have many fine qualities, *you must* change every aspect of your behavior that I dislike."

1. Do we ever behave like the inflexible chimpanzee? Do we hold on to rigid expectations of one another? Do we find it

difficult to consider alternate ways of doing things?

Let's talk about these questions.

2. Are we expecting perfection from one another? Or do we accept the fact that we both have flaws—and probably always will?

TIME TO TALK

Our differences are just that—differences. Differences do not mean that my ways are necessarily better than yours, or that my attitudes are good while yours are bad. It's like the story of the mountain and the squirrel who were arguing about which was superior. Finally, the squirrel said, "It's true that you can carry trees on your back, but I can crack open a nut."

Unfortunately, when our differences pop up we often lack the "serenity to accept the things I cannot change." Each of us seems to say "I know I have faults. I know I'm not perfect. But I want you to accept me as I am. On the other hand, I won't accept you as you are. You must change." If both of us adopt this rigid attitude we reach a stalemate. Hoping that the other will magically change usually gets us nowhere. Nothing constructive will happen unless one of us starts to ask:

"How am *I* contributing to our disagreements?"

"What can *I* do to make matters better?"

"How can *I* change?"

Changing myself

Do you know the words of that old spiritual,

" 'Taint my brother or my sister, but it's me, O Lord,
Standing in the need of prayer."

In a similar way, " 'taint" you that may need changing. It's probably me who stands in the need of some shaping up.

Let's consider a disagreement between Ann and Fred as a case in point.

Fred complained that Ann never wanted to go out in the evening. He accused her of being a "stick-in-the-mud, just like your mother." He blamed her for being too absorbed in the home and the children. He insisted that *she should change.*

When Ann was confronted with these accusations, she retorted, "Yes, it's true that I don't want to go out. But it's not because I'm so much in love with our home. It's because you drink way too much when we go out. And when you get high, I don't appreciate the nasty things you say about me to others. I feel humiliated. So I'd much rather stay at home."

After the usual interchange of defensive statements, Fred decided that *he* could do some changing.

Here's another example:

Chuck: When are you going to stop all that nibbling and snacking? You're getting as fat as a cow. You've got to do something about your weight.

Lynn: You don't have to remind me of my weight. Every time I try to squeeze into a dress I'm reminded of it myself. You know darn well I've tried to diet, but it's not easy.

Chuck: But you've got to do something about it.

Lynn: I know I've got to do something about it. You don't have to repeat it. But a few changes on *your* part would help me a lot. I've never told you this before, Chuck, but I've noticed that whenever I feel you're ignoring me, I turn irresistably to food. I feel that if you brought me a flower, or complimented me occasionally, or talked more to me instead of acting like an Egyptian mummy, I would turn to you instead of food. (Laughs) I'd rather reach out for a Chucky instead of a sweet.

Chuck took this suggestion under consideration. By changing himself he helped Lynn to change her eating habits.

Have I ever said to you, "You never listen to me. Whatever I say goes in one ear and out the other"?

Whenever you don't listen to me I feel irritated or ignored. I may want you to change and start listening to me. But instead of focusing all my attention on changing you, I might ask myself:

How am *I* contributing to the problem?
Are you turning off your hearing aid because *I'm* so critical of you?
Are you tuning me out because *I'm* making demands on you that you cannot meet?
Am *I* picking a poor time to speak to you?

I can go even further and ask myself:

What can *I* do to improve the situation?
Do *I* listen to you when you speak to me?
Could *I* pick a better time to talk to you, other than when you are listening to Walter Cronkite or just before you fall asleep or when you are busy getting the kids off to school?

Let's suggest a few ways in which both of us can make changes. Let's only make specific suggestions that are within the realm of possibility for changing.

TIME TO TALK

1. I will suggest two things that I would like *you* to do that I'd appreciate a great deal. I'll make these suggestions now before you read the next question.

2. Now I, your partner, will suggest two things that I would like *you* to do that I'd appreciate. I'll make these suggestions now before you read the next question.

Saturday Review

*"Don't ask me **how** you've failed me. I just feel it in my bones sort of."*

3. Now I'll tell you two specific ways in which *I* would like to change *my* behavior in order to improve our relationship.

4. Now I'll suggest two specific ways in which *I*, your partner, would like to change so that we can get along better.

Nondefensiveness—admitting my mistakes

One important way of changing myself is by striving to be less defensive when I talk to you. Nondefensiveness is the opposite of blaming, accusing, fault-finding, and making excuses. When I'm nondefensive, I "tell it like it is." I stand up and accept myself for what I am. I take responsibility for my thoughts and actions. Not only do I express myself more frequently through I COUNT messages and bad-mood warnings, but I also admit my mistakes and shortcomings.

I recognize that I'm an imperfect human being. I don't have angel's wings sprouting from my shoulder blades. I agree with

Alexander Pope that "to err is human." I'm not afraid to admit my faults and limitations.

Let's read a few examples of nondefensive communication.

She: I do drive faster than I should. I'll try to slow down a little.

He: I know that when I say, "I'm too tired for sex," it's a cop-out on my part. The least I could do is lie close to you in bed and snuggle with you.

She: I'm sorry I hurt you so much. There's no defense for what I've done. I was dead wrong.

He: I realize that my tone of voice does sound harsh and demanding. I must come across like a top sergeant.

Now we'll take turns expressing several nondefensive statements. In each statement we'll admit to a shortcoming on our parts. I'll start.

Changing you

How about changing you? Someone has said that marriage is not a reform school. This saying has a great deal of truth to it, particularly if I try to cajole, belittle, nag, or manipulate you into changing your ways. Lectures, harangues, and sermons often do not help either.

These standard techniques of persuasion usually fail because they simply do not take into account the fact that my intended message for changing you is not the same message that you may receive. What comes out of my pitcher isn't going into your glass.

For example, suppose I tried to persuade you to start hanging up your clothes in the closet instead of carelessly dropping them on a chair or on anything else that happens to be around.

The message I hope to convey is, "I wish you would start hanging up your clothes." But in order for you to change, you must also say to yourself, "Yes, I'd like to hang up my clothes."

Suppose, however, I reeled off, "When the hell are you going to stop being sloppy and start hanging your clothes up the way a grown person should? All I do is pick up around here."

Although my intended message may have been "I wish you'd start hanging up your clothes," what goes into your glass, that is, *what you may say to yourself* (even though it is not openly expressed), would be something like, "You may want me to change. But I feel under attack. I feel belittled. I feel that I DON'T COUNT." In all likelihood you would begin to bristle and react defensively. You'd resist my suggestions for change.

Our suggestions often are intended to stimulate changes in each other. We may have tried to persuade each other to improve our driving, cooking, manners, or some other form of social behavior.

Were these suggestions ever perceived as criticism, nagging, or attacks on each other's self-esteem? Did we change?

Let's discuss these questions.

The opera—words and music

Have we ever stopped to realize that our conversations often resemble what goes on in an opera? We speak words. But behind our words there is a great deal of "music." My words reveal *what* I am saying, but my music reveals *how* I'm saying it.

When I speak to you, what fills your glass is very much influenced by the way you interpret my words and my music.

For example, suppose you returned home one evening. I greeted you by saying, "I've been waiting for you. Where have you been?"

Let's assume that you clearly heard my words. But what sort of "music" will your glass be picking up?

You may have noticed the frown on my face when I greeted you. You also may have picked up the irritated tone in my voice. In addition, the fact that I turned my back on you when you came in hardly escaped your attention.

If such a greeting were to occur, what would my tone of voice and body language communicate to you?

Let's talk about this a moment.

TIME TO TALK

Now, suppose I had greeted you instead with a smile, a warm embrace, and a pleasant,but concerned tone, as I said, "I've been waiting for you. Where've you been?"

What would your glass have picked up from my pitcher now?

Let's discuss this before going on to the next section.

TIME TO TALK

The intended message and the accompanying message

We'll refer to the literal message we wish to convey as the *intended message.*

We'll call our body language, our tone of voice, and everything else that accompanies our intended message (including additional words), the *accompanying message.*

The main lyrics are the intended message, while the harmony and backup music constitute the accompanying message.

This notion of intended and accompanying messages is extremely important if I hope to persuade you to change.

If my intended message, for example, is "I wish you'd hang up your clothes," and my accompanying message is, 'You're such a sloppy pig," chances are your ears will pick up the latter YOU DON'T COUNT message more clearly than my intended message. Most likely my efforts to change you will produce nothing but a bitter argument.

But if my intended message, "I wish you'd hang up your clothes" is accompanied by a YOU COUNT message, "I realize that you have many other things on your mind," you'd be more prone to hear my intended message in an open, nondefensive way. The chances of your hanging up your clothes would be much greater.

Here is an illustration of the importance of sending YOU COUNT accompanying messages.

Ray, thirty-six, and Irene, thirty-five, have been married fourteen years. They have four children. They presented their problems to a counselor.

Ray, who worked in an auto assembly plant, felt under a great deal of tension at his job. In order to relax after work, he began dropping in to a local tavern for a "short beer." Unfortunately from Irene's point of view, he would arrive home quite late. She became increasingly irritated at his behavior. She berated him for keeping her and the four children waiting while dinner was getting cold.

The dispute escalated in typical fight-flight fashion, she attacking him and he defending himself. One evening, for example, Ray felt he couldn't tolerate any more YOU DON'T COUNT assaults. He yelled back and then stalked out of the house, tavern bound.

After a while, as a result of her counseling, Irene became convinced of the futility of her YOU DON'T COUNT efforts at reforming him. She then decided on a new approach. One morning, before he left for work, she addressed him in a relatively calm voice:

> You know how annoyed I get when you come home so late. The meal is cold. The kids and I miss you. (I COUNT, "I wish" message) We would so appreciate it if you came home earlier. (YOU COUNT message) But if you feel your short beer is so necessary to relax, *I would understand* your trip to the tavern, even though I don't like it one bit.

That evening, to her surprise, Ray returned home early!

What happened?

What happened to change Ray's behavior?

Irene's intended message, "I'd like you to come home early" remained the same. But the accompanying message had changed from YOU DON'T COUNT to YOU COUNT. And for the first time, Ray listened to her intended message in an open and non-defensive way. Before, in response to her YOU DON'T COUNT accusations, he'd been saying to himself:

> My wife is a battle-ax. She has a hell of a nerve yelling at me. If I feel like going to a tavern for a short beer, neither she nor anyone else can stop me.

Now he began saying to himself:

> I know I enjoy going to the tavern. But Irene's got a point. I really have a responsibility to her and the kids. I should try to get home earlier.

He later expressed himself in the following way:

> When I came home late, Irene used to cut me down. I felt bamboozled by her. I felt like a goose egg, like a nothing. I realized that fighting back didn't help, so I decided to hang around the tavern even more. Now I realize the drinks were anesthetics to escape from my work problems and from Irene. I was bowled over when she told me it was all right for me to have a few drinks. For the first time I felt I was not a goose egg or a naught. You know, it's funny when you come to think of it, *but the moment she stopped telling me what to do, I began listening to her.*

It may seem like a paradox, but the more I accept you as you are, the more open you'll be to suggestions for change.

In the above situation, Irene really was saying to Ray, "I would very much like you to change. But even if you don't, I'm ready to accept you as you are."

Of course, there's no 100 percent guarantee that this method of trying to change you will be successful at all times. But a YOU COUNT accompanying message will at least give you a greater opportunity to consider my proposals in a fair way. You'd be less hampered by defensiveness.

I COUNT—YOU COUNT messages

A highly desirable approach in our efforts at persuading each other to change is the use of I COUNT—YOU COUNT messages.

This type of message contains an I COUNT message as well as an accompanying message that essentially says, "YOU COUNT." It expresses how I feel as well as an indication that I understand or appreciate your viewpoint.

In most instances, this type of message begins with a YOU COUNT message and then is followed by an I COUNT message.

Here are a few examples:

She: (YOU COUNT message) I realize that you are under a great deal of pressure at the plant and that you need to unwind with a few beers after work. (I COUNT message) But I get awfully annoyed when the dinner gets cold and the kids and I have to wait for you. I wish you'd come home and unwind with us.

He: (YOU COUNT message) I can see that you are stuck in the house all week with the kids and want a chance to get out more and meet people. (I COUNT message) But I'm so dead tired from work today I just feel like taking it easy and watching TV tonight.

"No flowers. That means you want me to think you haven't got a guilty conscience."

She: (I COUNT message) I can't say I approve of your wish to drop out of school. (YOU COUNT message) But I certainly understand why you are thinking of doing it.

He: (YOU COUNT message) I realize that you've been in a bad mood all morning. (I COUNT message) But I would appreciate it if you'd stop turning on the vacuum cleaner and sit down and talk with me.

She: (YOU COUNT message) I realize that in your upbringing there wasn't much of a premium put on etiquette and social niceties. (I COUNT message) But I would love it if you brought home some flowers every now and then.

Let's take turns expressing three such I COUNT—YOU COUNT messages to each other. Let's remember that an I COUNT message usually begins with "I feel. . ." "I think. . ." or "I wish. . . ." A YOU COUNT message usually begins with, "I realize that. . ." "I can well understand it when. . ." "I appreciate it when. . ." or "I can see that. . . ."

I'll start by expressing one I COUNT—YOU COUNT message. Then we'll alternate until each of us has expressed three such statements.

Heads I win, tails you lose

One of the most discouraging experiences takes place when you accept my suggestions for change, but whenever you try to carry out my suggestions, I pour cold water on your efforts. Either I expect perfection or I persist in criticizing you despite your attempts to please me.

It's like the story of the wife who repeatedly urged her husband to express greater affection. One evening, when the husband came home, he greeted her with a friendly, "Hi, honey!" and then gave her a nice hug. To his utter surprise, she broke loose from his embrace and shouted,

"What a day it's been! Willy came in with a bloody nose. The cat threw up on the living room rug. The dishwasher broke down. And now you come home drunk!"

The husband probably got the feeling that he couldn't win no matter what he did.

Here are a few more examples of this "heads I win, tails you lose," double-bind dilemma:

Donna: I wish you'd phone during the day. It would give me a real charge to know that you're thinking of me.

Bob: (on the phone the following day) Hi, Donna! How are things? What are you doing with yourself?

Donna: Is this a sincere phone call? Are you trying to play games with me? Are you phoning because you really want to, or just because I suggested it?

Bill: You seem to find good things to say about everyone but me. Can't you ever compliment me?

Verna: (several mornings later) Gee, Bill, that was a wonderful omelette you made. I've never eaten anything as delicious.

Bill: (with indignation) Yeah, that's all I'm good for around here—a damned eggmaker.

Connie: Jack, you never make any suggestions for the whole family doing things together. You never think of all of us going out and enjoying ourselves.

Jack: (the following morning) Connie, I've got an idea. Why don't the whole bunch of us, you, I, and the kids, go out tonight and play some miniature golf?

Connie: (with sarcasm) A fine night you pick to have fun. You should know by now that Tuesday night is the night I do the washing.

Wouldn't it have been more desirable in the third example for Connie to have used an I COUNT—YOU COUNT message in response to Jack's suggestion?

Here's how it might have sounded. Let's read our parts again.

Connie: Jack, you never make any suggestions for the whole family doing things together. You never think of all of us going out and enjoying ourselves.

Jack: (the following morning) Connie, I've got an idea. Why don't the whole bunch of us—the kids, you, and I, go out tonight and play some miniature golf?

Connie: (I COUNT) Tonight's not the best night for miniature golf. I usually do the laundry on Tuesdays. (YOU COUNT) But I do appreciate the suggestion. How about taking the kids out tomorrow night?

What sort of I COUNT—YOU COUNT message would have been appropriate in the first example?

Let's reread the beginning of the dialogue between Donna and Bob. Then we'll pinch hit for Donna. Instead of reading her "heads I win—tails you lose" response, we'll substitute an I COUNT—YOU COUNT message in the blank spaces.

Donna: I wish you'd phone during the day. It would give me a real charge to know that you're thinking of me.

Bob: (on the phone the following day) Hi, Donna! How are things? What are you doing with yourself?

Donna: (I COUNT or YOU COUNT message) ____________

Now let's do the same for the second example.

Bill: You seem to find good things to say about everyone but me. Can't you ever compliment me?

Verna: (several mornings later) Gee, Bill, that was a wonderful omelette you made. I've never eaten anything as delicious.

Bill: (I COUNT or YOU COUNT message) ____________

An I COUNT—YOU COUNT conversation

Let's close this session with another "What do you hear me

saying?" type of conversation. From now on, though, we'll refer to it as the I COUNT—YOU COUNT conversation. Not only will we continue to use the "What do you hear me saying?" technique, but we'll make full use of the other I COUNT—YOU COUNT skills as well.

Here's an example of an I COUNT—YOU COUNT conversation between Paul and Melissa. They've been married twelve years. One weekend, Paul sensed that there was a great deal of tension in the air. He tuned in to his own feelings and discovered that he was quite upset and angry. That evening he suggested that he and Melissa hold an I COUNT—YOU COUNT conversation. Below is the beginning of their dialogue.

Paul: I'd like to bring up something that's been bothering me the last few days. Is it OK if we have an I COUNT—YOU COUNT conversation about it?

Melissa: That's fine with me. I have noticed you were acting sort of remote of late. What's on your mind?

Paul: *(I COUNT messages)* I've become very irritated with an attitude I feel you've been developing toward me. I get the feeling that I'm constantly living with a censor around here. The moment I enter the house I expect you to take me to task for one thing or another.

(YOU COUNT message) I realize that you may not feel this way or even be aware of it, (I COUNT message) but I feel as if you've decided to take charge of my behavior. I sense in you a constant disapproval of whatever I do. I've had this feeling for quite some time now.

What are you hearing me say?

Melissa: What I hear you saying, loud and clear, is that you are very annoyed with me. You seem to feel that I'm some sort of self-appointed censor, that every time you come home you expect some sort of disagreeable criticism from me. And this isn't something new. You feel this has been going on for quite some time.

(YOU COUNT message) I'm sorry you feel that way. I know. I've often felt that way also.

(I COUNT message) But I wasn't aware that I was hovering over you ready to pounce on you for any little thing. I really feel that I've made a deliberate effort to hold myself back from criticizing you. I guess my criticism of you is visible without my being aware of it.

Now, what do you hear me saying?

Paul: You're saying that you are not aware of your hovering over me and that you've cut down on being critical. If you've cut down on finding fault with me, I appreciate it. Maybe I should give you an example of what I mean. If we are with people and I tell a story and I'm boisterous and laughing, you seem to disapprove. It's another black mark in your book. Even though you don't say so openly I can see a frown of dissatisfaction on your face.

Melissa: (YOU COUNT message) I can see why you're so upset about it. (I COUNT message) But I think you are manufacturing a situation that doesn't exist. There have been many times when I've disapproved of your actions, but I've kept it to myself. It's definitely not my intention to hound you.

What am I saying?

Paul: You're saying, and I'm glad to hear it, that you don't intend to hound me. Maybe if you came out openly and said, "I disapprove of what you are doing" or something like that, rather than just thinking it, I wouldn't get that vague feeling of a cloud hanging over my head.

How do you read me?

 ***How to initiate an I COUNT—YOU COUNT conversation***

When we ask each other to hold an I COUNT—YOU COUNT conversation, it is highly desirable:

1. To *agree* on holding a conversation.
2. To *agree* on the *topic* of the conversation.
3. To *agree* on the *time* for the conversation.

If I were to invite you to hold an I COUNT—YOU COUNT conversation, it would probably never get off the ground if you weren't interested in holding one or if we couldn't agree on the time for it.

Let's consider this short interchange between Mary Lou and Gordon. It demonstrates an unsuccessful attempt at starting an I COUNT—YOU COUNT conversation.

Mary Lou: I'd like to have an I COUNT—YOU COUNT conversation with you about my mother's visit next month.

Gordon: For crying out loud! Can't you see I'm eating? I can't even enjoy a meal around here without you bringing up disagreeable subjects.

Mary Lou: I give up. I can't get you to talk about anything.

Mary Lou's efforts at holding an I COUNT—YOU COUNT conversation have failed because she and Gordon lacked agreement on when to hold it. She also may have picked the wrong time to broach the subject.

The second time around, their try was more successful.

Mary Lou: (I COUNT message) I've been worried about my mother's visit next month. I would very much appreciate having an I COUNT—YOU COUNT conversation about it. When do you think would be a good time to get together and talk it over?

Gordon: I didn't know it was bugging you. How about tonight after the kids have gone to bed?

Mary Lou: That's fine with me.

It's now our turn to hold an I COUNT—YOU COUNT conversation. Either one of us can start, on any topic we wish. Let's make a conscious effort to use I COUNT—YOU COUNT messages.

Wrapping up

This is the end of the sixth session.

Let's review some of the major points we've been discussing.

1. **We've been raised differently. We, therefore, differ in many of our present attitudes.**

2. **The greatest YOU COUNT gift I can give you is to accept you as you are, even though I do not approve of everything you say or do.**

3. **The first step toward constructive change is to ask myself:**
   "What am *I* doing that contributes to our difficulties?"
   "What can *I* do to improve the situation?" **and**
   "How can *I* change?"

4. **One important way of changing is by cutting down on my defensiveness. Through nondefensive communication I admit my mistakes and accept responsibility for my shortcomings.**

5. When I communicate, my words are my intended message, but the way I express myself, my tone of voice and my body language, make up my accompanying message.

6. If my accompanying message is YOU DON'T COUNT, you probably will react to my intended message in a negative and defensive way. However, if my accompanying message says YOU COUNT, you will most likely give greater consideration to my suggestions for change.

7. I COUNT—YOU COUNT messages are excellent ways of communicating. They express an understanding or appreciation of your point of view, as well as a declaration of how I feel and think.

8. The I COUNT—YOU COUNT conversation makes use of the "What do you hear me saying?" technique as well as other communication skills.

9. If we wish to get an I COUNT—YOU COUNT conversation started, it is desirable to agree on the topic and the time for the conversation.

Between sessions

Activity 1. Let's reread the session.

Activity 2. After the individual readings, let's have a short discussion about the material. Let's talk about how we can put some of the ideas to use in our daily living.

Activity 3. Then let's hold another I COUNT—YOU COUNT conversation. We can bring up any topic for discussion.

In initiating the conversation let's follow the suggestions made in the section, "How to initiate an I COUNT—YOU COUNT conversation." Again, let's try to cut down on attacking each other and defending ourselves. Let's use I COUNT—YOU COUNT messages as well as other communication skills.

After we've revealed our opinions and feelings through our I COUNT—YOU COUNT conversation, let's pause awhile and then say to each other,

"We've been expressing our feelings to each other. Now it's time to suggest some solutions. Each of us will answer these questions:

What can *both of us* do to improve the situation?
What can *I* do to improve the situation?

Have we tried:

a. A daily powwow or a daily ten-and-ten dialogue?
b. A daily YOU COUNT deed?
c. I COUNT—YOU COUNT messages in our daily living?

SESSION SEVEN
Four styles of communication

If we've reached this point in the program and have absorbed some of the major points, we deserve congratulations. Most likely our ability to communicate and relate to one another has improved considerably.

In this session we plan to talk about our different styles of communication. We'll also get a chance to review some of the basic ideas we've discussed so far.

Either one of us can start reading now.

The lump becomes a lamp

Have we ever noticed that we don't speak to everyone in the same way? I may shout at you, for example, but I wouldn't dream of bawling out my next door neighbor. My manner of speaking at a church board meeting probably differs from my style of conversing at home or at an office party.

Sometimes within a split second we can switch from a *private*, personal style to that of a *public* style of talking. A well known example is that of the mother who is scolding her noisy children. The phone rings. And then, as if by magic, the moment she picks up the receiver, her shrill voice is transformed into a warm, friendly "hello."

Sandra observed a similar transformation in her attorney husband. She remarked, "Joe could be sitting in the living room for hours like a lump. He acts tired, lackadaisical, and blah. All he does is grunt at us. But as soon as that phone rings and one of his female clients is on the phone, watch out. It's 'How are you, Nancy? Gee, it's so nice hearing from you.' The lump becomes a glowing lamp."

Drawing by Geo. Price; © 1963 The New Yorker Magazine, Inc.

"You had no trouble scintillating at the Martins'. Why can't you scintillate here?"

Four styles of communication

The two examples just given illustrate not only our public and private styles of conversing but also the amazing flexibility and adaptability we display in our daily communication.

The fact that we have a variety of communication styles at our disposal gives us hope that we can change and improve our ways of relating to each other. We can unlearn old, unproductive ways of acting and talking. We can learn new and more satisfactory ways of behaving.

We've probably observed changes and improvements in ourselves since the start of the program.

In this session we won't be concerned with the split-second shifts in our ways of conversing. We'll deal, instead, with the more enduring and more persisting styles of personal communication between us.

Below is a listing of four basic communication styles that describe our present relationship. We all use one or the other of these styles at different times. We may use several of them during the week.

All too often, however, one of these styles describes our *predominant* way of relating. It's up to us to determine which of the four styles fits us.

The four basic styles are:

1. **The I DON'T COUNT—YOU DON'T COUNT style.**
2. **The I DON'T COUNT—YOU COUNT style.**
3. **The I COUNT—YOU DON'T COUNT style.**
4. **The I COUNT—YOU COUNT style.**

We'll discuss each of these styles. As we do so, we'll also be reviewing much of the material we've covered in the program.

The I DON'T COUNT—YOU DON'T COUNT style

This style is a familiar one. Remember the cold shoulder, the silent treatment, and the "brother and sister act"?

In this style, we communicate by not communicating. Either we don't say much or we're totally indifferent to each other. Our I COUNT ladders are folded up and stored in separate closets. We live separate but parallel lives, like two goldfish in adjacent tanks. "The warm poetry of our marriage has changed to cold prose." We just go through the motions of being a couple.

One common pattern of this style is the "So what else is new?" relationship. This pattern is like a scene from the movie, *Marty*. One person asks, "What are you doing tonight, Marty?" Marty replies, "Nothing, what are you doing?" "Nothing," says the friend.

A similar style develops when we feel hopeless about our marriage. We are convinced that no matter what we do, nothing

"Apart from a joint bank account and a joint tax return. . . we seem to share no interests these days. . . ." © Punch

will change. Our attitude is, "It wouldn't make any difference anyhow, so why communicate?"

Marriage counselors have a name for couples living this sort of stagnant existence. They are called "gruesome twosomes." Gruesome twosome couples suffer from a severe case of "noncommunicativitis."

Other couples are perfectly capable of communicating, but because of widely different personalities or interests they find nothing to talk about. Rather than trying to find new interests and activities that they might share and discuss, they simply allow themselves to drift apart.

Here is how one bitter woman described her I DON'T COUNT—YOU DON'T COUNT marriage:

"When Bill and I first met, we were strangers. Then we fell in love and became intimate companions. Now we've drifted back into being strangers again."

Would the I DON'T COUNT—YOU DON'T COUNT style describe us in any way? Are we becoming strangers rather than intimate companions? If so, what do we think we can do about it?

The I DON'T COUNT—YOU COUNT style

In this style one of us takes an inferior, I DON'T COUNT position and acts it out repeatedly. If I happen to be the person in the I DON'T COUNT corner, I become the dog in the manger. I take the back seat. I discount myself and apologize for all my mistakes. I become a martyr.

I rarely express my displeasure or unhappiness. I lack the courage to speak up. I'm afraid to do anything that might ruffle your feathers.

If I'm the underdog, I make frequent use of I DON'T COUNT messages. Here are a few:

She: I always put my foot in it.

He: I guess I have no right to complain after all you've done for me.

She: When will I ever learn? I'm a real dum-dum.

He: As usual you are right. I keep making one mistake after another.

One woman declared to her husband, "For years I've been playing the doormat. I've let you step all over me."

Let's discuss these questions one at a time.

1. Is this a style that occurs between us? If so, who is usually the I DON'T COUNTer?

2. Do I tend to blame myself excessively? Do I often suffer in silence or indulge in self-pity, rather than speak out?

3. If I'm an I DON'T COUNTer, what can I do to boost my I COUNT?

TIME TO TALK

Do the rocks in my head fit the holes in yours?

The I DON'T COUNT—YOU COUNT style is a common one. We may go through our entire married life with one of us kowtowing to the other. If one of us feels comfortable in holding down the I DON'T COUNT end of the stick, then we have no great problem. "The rocks in your head fit the holes in mine" and we get along fine.

All too often, however, the rocks and the holes don't fit. Beneath the pleasant, submissive exterior of the I DON'T COUNTer there usually is a deep frustration. I may be smiling on the outside, but I'm gritting my teeth on the inside.

Many partners who slip into the I DON'T COUNT role pay dearly for their doormat status. Instead of tuning in and speaking out, their motto becomes, "Tune out and be quiet." As a result, their self-esteem takes a nose dive.

Psychiatric offices are filled with people who qualify as I DON'T COUNTers. Along with their lowered self-worth, they often stockpile within themselves a great deal of resentment toward their partners. They frequently suffer from symptoms of tension and depression. They become afflicted with psychosomatic ailments. Their bodies catch up with their emotions.

Often when an I DON'T COUNTer takes to a hospital bed, he or she really is communicating in body language. What is being said is, "In order to continue to live with you, I have to become ill or depressed. My illness is my desperate effort to force you to pay attention and have you realize that I COUNT also."

In many marriages, wives habitually bite their tongues and suffer in silence for the sake of harmony.

Judy, for example, put all her I COUNT eggs into the marriage basket. She was totally dedicated to pleasing her husband. She expected fidelity, protection, and security in return. But when her husband, Henry, deviated from the unwritten "protection and security" contract, she exploded. When Henry expressed a relatively mild interest in another woman, Judy rushed to her divorce lawyer. Although she didn't follow through on a divorce, she held on to a fixed, unbending hostility toward Henry. She refused to forgive or forget his "transgressions." She often would announce, "I can't stand you touching me." She rejected his sexual advances.

Judy's actions were saying, "For years I've been playing the doormat. But you've stepped on me once too often. It was the last straw. Now, through my coldness and hostility, I'm repaying you for my years of I DON'T COUNT. Now I'm wiping my shoes on you. From here on in, it's I COUNT—YOU DON'T COUNT."

Do these ideas have any personal meaning for ourselves? Let's discuss this.

"TIME TO TALK"

The I COUNT—YOU DON'T COUNT style

We referred to this style when we talked about fight-flight reactions earlier in the program. It's the style I may use whenever I feel hurt, rejected, or angry. I discount you in order to elevate my I COUNT.

A frequent variation on the I COUNT—YOU DON'T COUNT theme is seen in the "angry woman syndrome." Here, the wife is the opposite of the I DON'T COUNT woman. Her husband usually is the battered one. He plays the doormat, while her mission in life is to discount him.

Rosemary was a typical "angry woman." She was raised in a family where she felt ignored and unappreciated. Her father was overly critical, perfectionistic, and sometimes abusive. Rosemary once declared, "In my father's eyes, I could never measure up. I could never do anything right."

Rosemary also deeply resented the fact that her brothers seemed favored or pampered by her mother. As a youngster she was given the menial tasks to do, while "my brothers did nothing at all except strum the guitar and go to school." According to Rosemary, "I did all the work but my brothers got all the gravy."

Along with her bitterness and distrust of men, Rosemary grew up with a deep feeling of I DON'T COUNT. Even though her husband, Don, was a nice guy who leaned over backwards to please her, she repeatedly downgraded him. Like a bully, she inflicted on him the disapproval and rejection she experienced as a child.

1. Does this pattern of behavior have any personal meaning for ourselves in any way?

2. Can we give any examples of our own I COUNT—YOU DON'T COUNT behavior?

Let's talk over these questions before going on to the next section.

TIME TO TALK

Communication "don'ts"

Below is a list of some of the most common communication "don'ts" that flourish when an I COUNT—YOU DON'T COUNT style is in full swing. We hope that we are eliminating them from our communication.

These "don'ts" have several points in common. Each reflects a struggle for power between us. Behind each "don't" lurk battle cries of "I'm the good guy—you're the bad guy," "I'm going to win and you're going to lose," and "I'm right and you're wrong."

When we hurl these slams at each other, we usually get away from the main issues of our disagreement. We get lost in the thickets of defending ourselves and of blaming each other. The ultimate result is that we both wind up behind the eight ball.

Let's take turns reading the list of "don'ts" and the examples for each of them. After we read each example, we'll ask each other whether there's been a lessening of these negative exchanges between us. Our answers should give us a fairly good gauge of how our communication has improved.

1. *Not listening, tuning you out, ignoring you*

Do we listen more to each other?

2. *Belittling, blaming, finding fault with you*

He: If Mike drops out of school, you have no one to blame but yourself. You caused it all.

She: What a dumb thing to do. Can't you do anything right?

He: When will you ever learn to cook a decent meal?

Have we cut down on faultfinding and belittling?

3. *Attacking your personality, analyzing your character*

She: You're just a spoiled child. You've never gotten over the pampering you got as a child.

He: You're just like your domineering mother.

She: You're the most neurotic person I've ever had the misfortune of meeting. You're all "parent" and "child" and no "adult."

Do we attack or "analyze" each other's personalities less often than we used to?

4. *Threatening, demanding, and ordering*

She: You *must* do what I say—and no backtalk.

He: You'd better have dinner ready when I get home or you'll be minus one husband.

She: If you don't agree to an "open marriage," I'm heading straight for my lawyer.

Are we demanding less? Do we threaten each other less often? Are we less inclined to give orders?

5. *Using "always," "never," and "everytime"*

He: You're *always* saying the wrong thing.

She: You *never* listen to me. You're *always* buried in your book. *Everytime* I talk to you, you disappear behind the pages.

He: You make the same stupid mistake *every time.*

Are we doing this less?

6. *Judging, moralizing, and preaching to you*

She: You should be ashamed of yourself, using such vulgar words in public.

He: When will you ever grow up and act like a mature, responsible human being?

She: God will get you if you don't shape up.

Are we less judgmental of each other?

7. *Dredging up the past, using it as today's ammunition*

He: Look who's talking about honesty. You deceived me before we got married when you told me you never had sex before. I refuse to believe anything you tell me now.

She: How come you suddenly started to act decently now? Damn it, why didn't you do it ten years ago? For ten years you've been inconsiderate of me. Your niceness now will never make up for your past behavior.

Have we cut down on dredging up the past?

? 8. *Throwing in the kitchen sink*

These are statements that bring up all sorts of issues instead of sticking to the main point.

She: How can I respond to you sexually when you ignore me all day? Then you demand instant sex at night. Also, when are you going to shut the bathroom door when you go to the john? Your manners are atrocious. You're just like your father. When will you ever. . . ?

Do we do this less? Do we stick to the main issue more often?

? 9. *Closed-door statements*

These are statements that close the door to any further exploration of a subject. Instead of listening or trying to draw you out, these remarks cut you short and derail your attempts at expressing yourself.

She: I'm so damn mad at what your mother said to me this morning. I'm tired of biting my tongue and keeping my feelings to myself. When I'm with her, I can't be myself anymore.

He: (Closed-door statement) Why tell me about it? That's your problem, not mine. What do you want me to do—sit down and cry with you?

He: Those darn employees of mine. They're stealing me blind. I pay them good wages and they repay me by robbing me.

She: (Closed-door statement) I just don't want to hear anything about it. I have troubles enough of my own.

She: Jeff, this book I'm reading is terrific. I find it so stimulating. Just listen to this. . .

He: (Closed-door statement) Who wants to listen to that drivel? Don't you ever tire of reading those arty books? They're all a lot of hot air to me.

Are we making fewer closed-door statements?

10. *"You can't change" statements*

These are remarks that discourage any possibility for change or improvement. They are "terminal" statements that declare your hopelessness or the futility of trying to change. The words, "can't," "won't," and "never" are frequently used.

He: Since the year one, women have been inferior to men. Even the Bible says so. There's no use trying to act against God and nature.

She: You're exactly like your German father. Like father like son. What's the use. You can't buck up against a mule. You'll never be any different.

He: What can I do? You're a Scorpio. When a woman is a Scorpio, her husband may as well throw in the towel.

Are we making fewer "you can't change" statements?

11. Owning your feelings

This is when I do your thinking for you. "I know best what's in your mind."

She: You really don't want to take up skiing at your age. You know you'll tire of it and give it up in a few days.

He: You say that you love classical music. But you know deep down that you can't stand to listen to it.

Are we "owning" our own feelings more and each other's less?

12. *A few additional "don'ts" are:*

Interrupting you.

Monopolizing the conversation.

Saying, "There's nothing wrong," when I'm really upset over something.

Sticking the needle in where it hurts.

Can we think of any other communication "don'ts" that we'd like to cut down on? Let's talk about this.

Fights

When we live close together, we often act like two sticks. When we rub against each other, we produce friction. The smoke rises. The sparks fly. The fire blazes. We have a fight—a "noisy difference of opinion."

"We took your advice about never going to bed mad. We haven't been to bed in four days. Now what?"

A fight really is an expression of the I COUNT—YOU DON'T COUNT style in its most uninhibited form.

As we can well imagine, a fight is highly unpleasant. Unless we make up afterwards, a blow-up leaves us feeling tense, hurt, and angry. Even though we may walk away from the battlefield, the combat goes on in our heads (and stomachs). We continue to feel hurt and indignant while we think up new YOU DON'T COUNT accusations to fling at each other.

Most fights can be prevented if we hold an I COUNT—YOU COUNT conversation before our suppressed resentments percolate too long within us. If we are given a chance to express ourselves fully and listen attentively to each other, there is no need to fight.

However, a fight may sometimes take place despite our best intentions. The objective then is to try to convert the fight into a positive experience that would bring us closer together.

Sometimes a fight may even be desirable. Giving our emotions a chance to "hit the fan" can clear the air, *provided:*

a) the fight produces *emotional relief* rather than *emotional overkill,* and

b) we pick up the pieces afterwards and *make up* in some constructive way.

A fight gives emotional relief when my major emphasis is on I COUNT, that is, on giving free expression to my frustrated and "hurt inside" feelings.

A fight produces emotional overkill when my aim is to be victorious over you by demolishing you. When I concentrate on belittling, insulting, and punishing you, my main emphasis is on YOU DON'T COUNT. When I hurl one communication "don't" after another at you it is unlikely that a fight will bring us closer together. It will only lead to further YOU DON'T COUNT exchanges.

Making up—the breakthrough

A crucial point in the positive resolution of a fight-flight situation takes place when one of us has the gumption to rise above hurt feelings and make a conciliatory move towards the other.

It takes courage to make that first YOU COUNT move. Unfortunately, many of us are too weak to do it.

Each of us says, "You've hurt me. You should make the first move. It's your turn to apologize. I'm afraid that if I make the first move and reach out, you'll reject me." Instead of making up, the way boxers do after a fight, we remain in our separate corners and simmer inside.

We'll try out a simple exercise in breaking through.

Let's stand up, back to back, with our arms folded. Let's do this now.

(After we've stood up, I'll continue to read.)

Let's pretend we've just had a fight. We're now giving one another the cold shoulder. Each of us feels angry, hurt, and ignored by the other. Let's stay in this cold shoulder position for a full thirty seconds. We'll count to ourselves. When the thirty seconds are up either one of us can take the initiative to turn around and embrace the other.

Let's do this now. (I'll put the book down and fold my arms.)
(After we've embraced, we'll go on.)

Have we ever had such an experience, where we broke through a hurt-angry, cold shoulder standoff?

Let's talk about it.

What happened? Who took the initiative to break the barrier and reach out? How did it feel?

Tea for two

One woman's prescription for ending a fight was, "Right in the middle of a fight I offer my husband a cup of coffee."

A cup of coffee in the middle of a fight may not be everyone's "cup of tea." But many couples find that an invitation to a snack or a cup of coffee *after* a fight has subsided is an important step in breaking the ice and making up.

Some couples need an initial cooling-off period away from one another. This can be followed by a talk session. A few husbands and wives prefer walking around the block, alone, before making a conciliatory move. Others find that a trip to the supermarket, or playing the piano, or having a crying spell is helpful before they can bury the hatchet.

During a cooling-off period, it may help also if we were to write "poison pen" letters to each other. In my letter I can write down, in a completely uninhibited way, whatever angry or hurt feelings I'm experiencing. I can make free use of four-letter words as I pour out my angry thoughts in writing. I never mail the letter, of course, nor do I show it to you. After reading it over a few times, I destroy my letter.

Another way of letting off steam is to drive alone in the car, in a safe, low-traffic area. I roll up the windows and then let things out, by giving free vent to my feelings. I yell and curse at the one who has "hurt" me.

1. How do we feel about any of the above suggestions for cooling off, letting off steam, and making up?

Are they worth trying?

2. What would be a good way for us to make up after we have had a fight?

TIME TO TALK

Bump, press, snarl, and flap

Making up after a fight brings us closer. Sometimes the increased intimacy after a fight can be highly exhilarating.

Encounter groups sometimes participate in "games" or exercises which simulate a fight, followed by an affectionate making up. The exercises often are entirely physical and non-verbal. They resemble what animals go through during courtship. First, there's a lot of physical commotion. This is followed by an embrace or some other form of affectionate reunion.

Here are four such exercises. Let's try them out, just for fun.

1. *Bumping shoulders*. We stand with our arms folded. We then vigorously bump our left shoulders. (In order to equalize our strength, the stronger one of us can stand on one foot during the bumping.)

Let's stand up and try it. After we bump each other, we'll embrace.

2. *Pressing hands*. We stand facing each other. We then extend our arms toward each other and interlock hands and fingers. With our arms in a stiff position, we press against one another in a vigorous fashion.

Again, after we've pressed hard against each other, we'll embrace.

3. *Snarling.* **We'll have to get down on our hands and knees for this. Now that we are down on the floor, let's pretend we're angry cats facing each other and start hissing, snarling, and grimacing.**

After a few seconds of tomcat noise-making, we'll get off the floor and embrace.

4. *Flapping.* **We face each other with our clenched hands close to our chests. We then flap our arms and make bird-like noises. Then we'll embrace.**

Let's discuss the questions below one at a time.

1. What do we think of the following idea? Whenever either one of us feels angry or upset, we can announce to the other, "I feel angry (or tense, or hurt). Let's fight it out." Then we can either bump, press, snarl, or flap at each other. This can then be followed by an affectionate making up.

2. Does either one of us feel the need for a *physical* release of tension?

3. Can we suggest any other method that might help us give vent to our hurt and angry feelings, followed by a making-up?

TIME TO TALK

After the fight is over—an I COUNT—YOU COUNT conversation

An excellent way of resolving a fight is to hold an I COUNT—YOU COUNT conversation. During our discussion, we can talk about the fight and explore the issues that led to our disagreement.

"Are you still mad, or am I again the only woman you'd like to be marooned on an island with?" ROTHCO

Here is the start of an I COUNT—YOU COUNT conversation.

Like most partners, Gloria and Bruce have their misunderstandings.

Gloria: (Initiating the conversation) I've been very upset over the fracas we had. I'm tired of our giving each other the silent treatment after a fight. I'd like to have an I COUNT—YOU COUNT conversation about our squabble. Is that OK with you?

Bruce: That's OK with me. Do you want to talk now?

Gloria: Yes. I was very upset about the weekend party we had. I had looked forward to having such a good time. I spent most of the day getting the house ready. Everybody was in a festive mood in the evening. When you walked in, I was really glad to see you, even though you came home late. But I felt hurt when you greeted everybody effusively and you didn't say "boo" to me. The same thing happened later in the evening when you and Joe were in the den. When I brought in those flowers to put in a vase, you shut up like a clam. To me, it was an indicator that you were discussing our personal problems with Joe—which I know you've done in the past. It was pretty obvious you didn't want me to hear what you were discussing. I was very hurt. I felt like an outcast, as if I were a virus or something.

Now, what do you hear me saying?

Bruce: You were very upset because I didn't include you in my greeting when I arrived at the house. I'm very sorry you felt that way. But I had the same reaction when I spoke to you. You merely looked at me. You didn't comment or welcome me home or anything like that. I felt really hurt. I'm sorry you felt so bad when my conversation with Joe ended when you came into the den. We weren't discussing our problems at all.

Now, what do you hear me saying?

Gloria: My interpretation of what appeared to me to be an embarrassed silence was all wrong.

Bruce: Yes—and I thoroughly enjoyed the evening. I thought that you did too, even though we didn't speak to each other much. I thought we were getting along well because we were acting like co-hosts. We naturally directed our attention to other people. I was deeply hurt, more deeply hurt than I could tell you, when you told me, about 10 o'clock in the evening, that I hadn't been civil to you all evening.

Gloria: (YOU COUNT message) I can well understand how you'd feel hurt about it if these were your genuine thoughts. Perhaps it's a carry-over from the past when you used to ignore me. (I COUNT message) But it hurts me inside to see other couples act so affectionately. They call each other pet names in front of us. There's no reason why we can't do the same in front of them. Just because there are people around, it doesn't mean we have to give each other the cold shoulder. Joe leans over and kisses Ellie on the forehead and ruffles her hair. Jim calls Edith "dear" every other sentence. I'd love it even if you passed on to me a pleasant little remark or feeling that showed you were aware that I was in the room. (Starts to cry) I can't help it. I feel so terribly hurt.

Bruce: (reaches over and places his arm around her) I guess you've been feeling lousy because I haven't been affectionate.

Gloria: (sobbing) I don't care about a lot of affection. I just want a little common courtesy. I don't insist on any physical demonstration. Just stop those cutting, sarcastic remarks, or not talking to me. I could even take your cutting remarks as a joke if I knew you were basically with me and showed me that in your eyes. I want you to show me that I COUNT. . . .

Let's go ahead and hold an I COUNT—YOU COUNT conversation of our own. Let's discuss some disagreement we've had recently. Let's remember to say "What do you hear me saying?" and try to listen and understand each other's point of view.

Either one of us can initiate the conversation.

Wrapping up

These are some of the main points we've discussed in Session Seven:

1. **Our styles of communication vary. We have our public as well as our personal styles of expressing ourselves.**

2. **The I DON'T COUNT—YOU DON'T COUNT personal style takes place when we lose interest or ignore each other. We become a "gruesome twosome."**

3. **The I DON'T COUNT—YOU COUNT personal style is one in which I take an inferior, subordinate position to you. I blame myself. I suffer in silence and feel sorry for myself. I allow myself to become a doormat in order to avoid disagreements and obtain emotional security. However, my suppressed anger may lead to a number of physical and psychological problems.**

4. **The I COUNT—YOU DON'T COUNT personal style is the familiar fight-flight reaction way of communicating. We defend ourselves excessively. We belittle and find fault with each other. We constantly stick pins into each other's self-esteem. We employ such communication "don'ts" as attacking each other's personality, blaming each other, and dredging up the past.**

5. **Fights are desirable when they provide emotional relief and when we make up afterwards. Fights are destructive when they lead to emotional overkill.**

6. **"Bump," "press," "snarl," and "flap" are good nonverbal ways of releasing angry feelings and clearing the air.**

7. A good way of resolving a fight or flight reaction is to hold an I COUNT—YOU COUNT conversation.

Between sessions

Activity 1. Let's reread Session Seven.

Activity 2. After our individual readings let's take some time out to discuss the material. Let's try to put some of the ideas into practice in our daily living.

Activity 3. Let's hold another I COUNT—YOU COUNT conversation during the week. Rather than discussing a problem that has developed between us, let's discuss the subject, "What can we do to further improve our relationship?"

Again, in initiating the discussion, let's first *agree* on whether we wish to hold a conversation on the suggested topic. Also, let's agree on the *time* for holding the conversation.

After the conversation, let's ask ourselves such questions as:

Did we stick to the main issue without becoming too defensive?
Did we ask each other, "What do you hear me saying?"
Was it a worthwhile conversation?
Are we making conscious efforts to use I COUNT—YOU COUNT messages in our daily conversations?

SESSION EIGHT

I COUNT—YOU COUNT

We're rounding third base. We're now about to go through our last session. We've already come a long way together. The chances are good that the time spent in the program has been worthwhile.

Again, let's sit close so that we can share the book. Either one of us can begin.

The I COUNT—YOU COUNT style

Throughout the book our main theme has been that happiness between us can best be achieved when we develop an I COUNT—YOU COUNT relationship. The I COUNT—YOU COUNT style of communicating helps us to achieve this goal.

In the I COUNT—YOU COUNT style, we employ the skills we've covered in the previous sessions. They were described mainly in the "Tune in an speak out," "YOU COUNT," and "Changing me—changing you" sessions. We'll now review many of these skills.

We'll name each skill and then read a few examples of its use. After each set of examples is read, we'll take turns giving additional examples of the particular skill. We should feel free to speak out on any subject we wish.

I COUNT—tuning in to myself and speaking out

? 1. *I COUNT, "I think" messages—expressing my thoughts and ideas.*

She: I think we should cancel the subscription. We're just throwing money away on this magazine.

He: I strongly disagree with you on how to discipline the children.

(Now, let's give our own examples.)

2. *I COUNT, "I feel" messages—expressing my feelings.*

Drawing by Saxon; © 1970 The New Yorker Magazine, Inc.

"Do you, Walter, promise to love and cherish, to make every effort to relate to a compatible life style, and to communicate on all meaningful levels?"

He: I feel awfully lonely when you're gone.

She: Whenever we go to these parties of academic people, the conversation makes me feel like a dummy.

He: I feel utterly delighted when you propose we go camping.

(Now let's give our own examples.)

3. *I COUNT, "I wish" messages—expressing my wishes.*

He: I'd like to get this matter settled once and for all.

She: I wish you'd stop pussyfooting around and come right out with what's really bothering you.

He: I wish we could spend more time together, instead of inviting people over so much.

(Now, let's give our own examples.)

4. *I COUNT, "hurt inside" messages—expressing my hurt feelings.*

He: I feel hurt inside whenever you criticize me.

She: I feel like crying when I don't hear from you.

He: I feel embarrassed when you drink in public.

(Now let's give our own examples.)

5. *Bad-mood warnings—letting you know when I'm in a bad mood.*

He: I'm just too upset to talk right now. I just feel terrible. I'd rather talk to you later.

She: I got a phone call from my sister this morning that was very upsetting. I don't know whether to scream or cry. You'd better keep away from me. Or better still, I could use a little sympathy and understanding.

He: Everything's gone wrong today. I'm in a lousy mood. Just don't bug me. Don't even look at me cross-eyed. If you do I'll bite your head off. I know I'm the villain, but that's just how I feel right now.

(Now let's pretend we're in a foul mood and give our own bad-mood warnings.)

 6. *Nondefensiveness—admitting my shortcomings.*

She: I've never had much training in expressing my feelings. I sit on them. That's why I withdraw when I'm angry at you. I've never learned to stick up for myself.

He: I guess I'm the exact opposite. There are many times when I wish I didn't shoot my mouth off so much. I should think first before spouting off.

She: I have a bad habit of ignoring you when you're talking. My mind drifts off and I start thinking of something unrelated to what you're talking about. I guess I'm self-centered that way. I should try to listen more.

(Now let's each of us express ourselves in a nondefensive way by admitting to our own shortcomings.)

YOU COUNT—tuning in to you and speaking out

1. *Positive strokes—expressing praise, understanding, or appreciation.*

She: It was awfully nice of you to take time out and phone me at work. It was my first day on the job. I appreciated your thoughtfulness.

He: It's great when you tell me what turns you on when we have sex. Not only do I enjoy sex more, but you become a much more exciting person in my eyes.

She: You were terrific when you said, "I'm not going to be a Scrooge and a grouch today. I'm going to be happy." You really counted in my book when you said that.

(Now let's give ourselves a few positive strokes.)

2. *"What do you think?" questions—asking about your thoughts and feelings on a particular subject.*

She: You've been awfully quiet lately. Could you tell me what's on your mind?

He: I'm anxious to get the house painted before we leave on vacation. What do you think?

She: I just can't make up my mind about whether I should go back to school this fall. How do you feel about it?

(Now let's give our own examples.)

3. *"What do you hear me saying?" questions—asking you to put yourself in my shoes by paraphrasing what I've said.*

She: I think it's unfair for me to work all day and then do all the household chores. I think you should help out with the work around the house. Now, what do you hear me saying?

He: You're always advocating togetherness. But I feel you carry it too far. I enjoy a night out with my pals now and then. I don't want to give them up just because we're married. What am I saying to you?

(Let's respond to each other's "What do you hear me saying?" questions.)

4. *YOU COUNT messages—letting you know that I understand how you feel, that I can put myself in your shoes.*

She: I can really understand why you're so tired when you come home.

He: I know how you feel. I don't blame you for being teed off at me.

She: I don't quite see it your way. Could you explain it a little more so that I can understand?

(Now let's give our own examples.)

***I COUNT—YOU COUNT* messages**

She: (YOU COUNT message) I can understand why you're having such a tough time kicking the habit. (I COUNT message) But I just can't stand all that smoke around the house.

He: (I COUNT message) I get annoyed when you say that. (YOU COUNT message) But I really appreciate it when you come right out with your feelings and tell me what's on your mind.

(Now let's give our own examples.)

Has there been an increase in our use of I COUNT—YOU COUNT messages?

Let's discuss this awhile.

The I COUNT—YOU COUNT attitude

Throughout the entire program we've been advocating an attitude of I COUNT—YOU COUNT. Our future happiness depends on how well we put this basic attitude into practice.

At this point we'd like to describe a specific I COUNT—YOU COUNT attitude in regard to *our anger* and *our differences.*

It's an attitude in which I realize that we differ in many ways. I do not expect our I COUNT ladders to mesh like well-lubricated gears. I recognize and accept the fact that we are both imperfect, fallible human beings. We often make mistakes. We get angry and express negative thoughts. Yet I feel we have a right to be angry at times, and that there is nothing wrong in expressing our anger.

We can break this attitude down into three parts:

1. **(I COUNT.) I respect and accept my own thoughts and feelings, including those of inadequacy, hurt, and anger.**
2. **(YOU COUNT.) Although we share many traits in common, I respect and accept the ways in which we differ. This includes an acceptance of your right to feel frustrated and angry, as well as your right to let me know about your upset state.**
3. **(The "hurt inside.") I realize that your anger and frustration often means that you have a "hurt inside."**

The I COUNT—YOU COUNT attitude toward our differences and our anger can be summed up in this I COUNT—YOU COUNT message:

"I may not like your behavior at times, but I respect your right to differ from or to be angry with me. At the same time, I respect my right to differ from you and to express my angry feelings to you (preferably through I COUNT messages)."

This attitude has a great deal of significance for us. Why don't we reread this section before going on.

The I COUNT—YOU COUNT attitude operates in the following way. Let's say we've just had an angry exchange of words. Right now I feel upset and hurt. But as soon as I calm down a little, I start thinking along these lines:

1. **(I COUNT.) We've just had an unpleasant disagreement. *I have a right to feel hurt and angry.* I don't feel guilty about my anger. If I wish, I can come right out and tell you, "I feel hurt," or "I feel angry."**
2. **(YOU COUNT.) I recognize that *you also have a right to be angry with or to disagree with me.* Even though I'm annoyed with you, I wish that you'd say to me, "I'm angry with you." It's no crime. It's perfectly normal and human.**
3. **(The "hurt inside.") I also realize that when we are angry, we're really *"hurting inside."* Being aware that we're both hurting, I become less defensive. I start to see you not as a hostile, attacking, snubbing person, but as more of a frustrated, unhappy, hurt person, struggling to maintain self-worth.**

If I adopt the I COUNT—YOU COUNT attitude, I will feel less hurt, less angry, and less vindictive. My anger will pass more quickly. I then can reach out to you more easily in a loving way.

After completing the program, a number of couples have revealed how gratified they were in taking on the I COUNT—YOU COUNT attitude.

Here is how Laura and Harvey viewed it:

Laura: You know, there's been a big change in the way we exchange angry words these days. Before, we'd yell at each other. Afterwards, we'd fester inside. Just a little bit of the anger would be expressed, like the tip of an iceberg showing. I'd have a lot of leftover anger. It would build and build. It was like nurturing a garden full of weeds inside me. It would wear me out. Besides, I'd only feel guilty for having expressed my anger.

Now I feel freer to get angry. It's not so much a matter of getting it all out, but of feeling comfortable about getting some of it out, and then accepting it and not feeling guilty about it. I've learned to accept my anger. As a result, I've begun to accept yours. Now, after a fight, I let things rest, instead of having it bubble and get worse.

Harvey: For me, too, the outcome of our angry words is different. Instead of intensifying the cold war, it's more like blossoms in the spring. We seem so much more comfortable with the anger in us and in coming out with it. It's funny. Before, you would ask, "Are you angry with me?" And I'd answer, "No. I'm not angry." Now I answer, "Maybe I am." Who knows, someday I'll say, "Yeah, darn tootin' I'm angry!"

Jeff and Beverly put it this way:

Jeff: I've found it very helpful to express my feelings more openly to you, especially when I accept these feelings. It doesn't have to be a complicated thing that I say to you. It could be a simple sentence. When I tell you, "I'm angry with you" or "I feel depressed this morning," it relieves these feelings inside me. I also feel that my remarks are perfectly normal. I no longer feel that I should be condemned for having them or expressing them. Expressing myself this way is like missing the bus. I may curse out the driver, but I don't feel hurt deep down because I cursed him. I accept my anger at you more and more, in the same way that I accept my anger at the bus driver.

The same is true about our lovemaking. When I give you an I COUNT message like, "I feel sexually frustrated when you are not in the mood," it doesn't snowball. I don't feel so mortally wounded when you turn me down.

Beverly: It's helped me a lot to be able to accept your statements about being angry or depressed or frustrated. For example, when you tell me that you're disappointed when we don't make love, my attitude is not guilt anymore. I don't feel that I've done anything wrong. I don't have the feeling that I'm short-changing you.

My attitude toward your displeasure is mainly, "What do I hear you saying?" even though I don't ask it out loud. And what I hear you saying is that you are angry and hurt, not that I'm to blame. Then I say to myself, "I don't feel in the mood today, but I'll probably feel like making love tomorrow." I really should come right out and say it to you.

To what extent have we developed an I COUNT—YOU COUNT attitude? Are we more accepting of our angry feelings and of our differences? Let's talk about this key question before going on.

I'm right—you're wrong, I win—you lose

The I COUNT—YOU COUNT attitude is particularly helpful in resolving specific differences and in solving problems. Let's compare the I COUNT—YOU COUNT approach with that of the I COUNT—YOU DON'T COUNT method.

Saturday Review

"You have a lot of annoying habits. . . just to annoy me, right. . . ?"

The I COUNT—YOU DON'T COUNT attitude harks back to our childhood. As kids we used to scream, "I'm right and you're wrong." As adults we often carry on in the same tradition. Whenever we differ on any subject, my goal is to convince you that my views are superior to yours.

Of course there are occasions when one of us is right and the other wrong. For example, if I insisted that the capital of Italy is Rome, and you contended it is Milan, I could, eventually, convince you that I am right. But usually, our personal disputes are not that simple. There may even be times where I can be "right" in a particular situation but I would be dead wrong in persisting on being "right." For example, I may have the right-of-way at an intersection. But suppose another driver is approaching the intersection at a right angle to me. He ignores his stop sign and is about to drive into my path. Obviously, I'd be a fool to continue driving and crash into him. At that moment, *what is right for both of us* (that is, the need to avoid the crash) is more important than my individual "right" to drive straight ahead.

In the same way, what is right for both of us often is more important than "I'm right and you're wrong." Both of us usually lose out when each insists on being "right."

Take this "my ideas count—you're ideas don't count" interchange as an example of how we can both lose out.

Jill: Did you see Jeff's report card? He's doing poorly in arithmetic again.

Jack: Yeah, I saw it. Why the hell don't you check over his arithmetic homework the way you're supposed to? Maybe if you helped him with his homework he'd pass some of the tests.

Jill: Okay, wise guy. If you're so eager for him to pass, why don't you help him? You're the mathematical genius around here.

Jack: Damn it, you know I don't have the time. It's your job anyway. Instead of spending hours coffee klatching with the neighbors you could spend a few minutes helping Jeff.

Jill: What do you mean "It's my job anyway"? What's wrong with *you* helping him? You're his father, aren't you?

Jack: I should hope so. I work damn hard to support this family. The least *you* could do is help Jeff do his arithmetic.

This is a fairly typical "I'm right—you're wrong" conversation. Each person is busy defending, attacking, and exchanging insults. Instead of confronting the issue, they confront each other. In the meantime, poor Jeff will continue to struggle with his fractions.

How different would this interchange have been if Jack and Jill had made an effort at understanding instead of belittling one another?

Below is an illustration of how that same issue could have been resolved if Jack and Jill had stuck to the problem and had used an I COUNT—YOU COUNT conversational style.

The dialogue starts the same way. But let's observe how it changes as soon as an I COUNT—YOU COUNT approach is used.

Jill: Did you see Jeff's report card? He's doing poorly in arithmetic again.

Jack: Yeah, I saw it. Why the hell don't you check over his arithmetic homework the way you're supposed to? Maybe if you helped him with his problems he'd pass some of his tests.

Jill: Why don't we have an I COUNT—YOU COUNT conversation on this problem? Is that OK with you?

Jack: It's fine with me. What did you hear me saying?

Jill: You were saying that you're mad at me and you're blaming me for Jeff's poor arithmetic grades.

Jack: (I COUNT messages) Yes. That's exactly how I feel. I'm worried about Jeff flunking.

Jill: (I COUNT messages) I'm worried too. I've tried to help him, but this newfangled arithmetic is Greek to me. I just cannot make head or tail out of it. So I've given up on it. I just don't know what to do. What do you think about it?

Jack: I don't know beans about this new math either. Why don't we speak to his teacher? Maybe she'll have some ideas.

Jill: Sounds like a good idea. We've just got to help Jeff somehow. I'll arrange to have a talk with her.

How much is 2 plus 2?

When faced with differences in attitudes and wants, some people are *problem solvers* while others are *problem producers.* Which are we?

There's an old joke about the difference between a normal, a neurotic, and a psychotic person.

If you ask the normal person, "How much is 2 plus 2?" he answers, "4."

If you ask the same question of the psychotic, he answers, "5."

But if you pose this problem to the neurotic, he replies, "I know that 2 plus 2 is 4, but *it makes me feel so nervous.*"

Many couples are in the same boat as the neurotic when it comes to solving problems and resolving differences. They are perfectly capable of getting the correct answer to "2 plus 2," or of working out their personal disagreements. Unfortunately, they permit their "nervousness," that is, their defensiveness, their rigidities, and their threatened self-worth to interfere with their achievement of a satisfactory solution.

Shrimp versus pizza

Let's take another problem. Let's observe how Harry and Sylvia, two *problem producers,* deal with it.

One evening they decide to eat out. Sylvia would like to have a shrimp dinner at the Seven Seas Restaurant, while Harry prefers a pizza at Gino's. Immediately after they make their preferences known, the following I COUNT—YOU DON'T COUNT interchange takes place:

Harry: Don't you get tired of eating shrimp all the time? You must think I'm made of money. You'll be ordering lobster next.

Sylvia: When I eat out I want something special—not a crummy pizza. Boy, do you have low taste in food.

Harry: I bring the dough into this house. It's my money, so it's going to be my taste. It's about time you appreciated what I do for you.

Sylvia: Spoken like a true male chauvinist. Don't you think I deserve some appreciation too? I've been preparing meals the way *you* like them for years. It's about time we eat where *I* like.

Harry: Let's skip the damn restaurant altogether. You can always pull a TV dinner out of the freezer.

Sylvia: You can go you know where. And where you're going there ain't no freezers.

Harry: The same to you.

Sylvia and Harry haven't resolved the pizza versus shrimp problem. Instead, their exhange of YOU DON'T COUNT messages has produced a new problem. Now they feel hurt, indignant (and hungry).

How would we have resolved this mighty shrimp versus pizza issue if it occured with us?

Let's discuss this.

Aileen and Al are *problem solvers*. They don't insist on "I win—you lose" or "you must agree completely with me." Their attitude is essentially I COUNT—YOU COUNT. They show respect for each other's I COUNT ladder and try to work out some realistic solutions.

When faced with a shrimp versus pizza dilemma their conversation may go like this:

Al: Aw, come on Aileen. We haven't had a pizza in ages. Why don't we try Gino's? You'd like their salad.

Aileen: I know that you'd love a pizza. But why don't we go to the Seven Seas this time and next week we'll give Gino's a whirl? Or if you insist, we can go to Gino's tonight and we can have shrimp next week.
What do you think?

Or it can sound like this:

Al: I wonder if there's some place in town where we can get a good pizza and a shrimp plate too?

Aileen: That's a good idea. I'll tell you what. I haven't seen Betsy in a long time. Why don't we phone her and Ed and have dinner where they want to go. Or maybe Betsy and I could go to the Seven Seas while you and Ed can wallow in pizza.

Al: I'll go you one better. Let's take them to a shrimp and pizza place. How about that?

Aileen: Fine. I'll phone Betsy.

An I COUNT—YOU COUNT conversation—problem solving

Our last illustration of an I COUNT—YOU COUNT conversation involves Mary and Joe, a couple who were seeing a marriage counselor.

Before the start of counseling they had built a huge wall between them. Not only were they not on speaking terms with one another, but they had been sleeping in separate bedrooms for the past three years! It all began over a dispute about the bedroom night light.

Joe claimed he had difficulty falling asleep. At first he tried to read in the living room until his eyes became tired. But as soon as he got into bed he seemed wide awake again. It was only when he turned on the bedroom night light and read in bed that he was able to doze off.

Although this seemed to solve Joe's sleeping problem, it brought one on for Mary. She protested that the light prevented

"—and, of course, I'm always very careful not to do anything that might antagonize her."

her from sleeping. She stated that she'd be lying in bed, three-quarters asleep, when in would walk Joe. He'd snap on the light and she'd awaken. One evening when this happened, Mary couldn't take it any longer. She angrily accused him of being selfish and inconsiderate. Then she stomped out of the bedroom and retired to their daughter's room, where she had been sleeping the past three years.

After two months of counseling they agreed to hold an I COUNT—YOU COUNT conversation on this problem.

Let's read our respective parts of a brief portion of the end of the conversation.

Mary: (responding to Joe's "What do you hear me saying?" question) You're wondering if we can go back to the old system again—you read in bed while I try to fall asleep. I doubt very much whether it'll work. It didn't then. Just when I'm about to fall asleep, you come in and turn that damn light on. I just get mad as hops when you do that.

I really have no suggestion. I'm stumped. What do you think?

Joe: (YOU COUNT message) I can understand your getting sore at me for turning on the light (I COUNT message), but I also was sore at you. I work darn hard all day and I just have to get a good night's sleep. When I tried to read in the living room, it didn't work. I wonder if we could make another stab at it. I'll try to read in the living room and then try to fall asleep in the bed.

Mary: I'll tell you what! I just got a wonderful idea. I think I can buy a set of blinders to put over my eyes while you read in bed. I saw a pair at the drug store the other day. It only costs about five dollars. Why don't I try it out and see how it works?

Joe: Sounds like a damn good idea.

They tried out Mary's suggestion. Mary moved back into their bedroom and put on the blinders. It worked! Then, to his surprise, Joe discovered that he was able to fall asleep *without* having to turn on the bedroom light. When the previous fight-flight tug of war was replaced by an attitude of I COUNT—YOU COUNT, the issue seemed to evaporate.

With good communication, most problems can be handled. We listen more. We're less defensive. We are more honest. Our minds are open to new courses of action and new solutions.

Before we end our last session, let's hold one more I COUNT—YOU COUNT conversation. This time let's have a discussion about any one of the following topics:

1. The good things about our marriage.
2. Several happy experiences we've had together.
3. Problems in the past that we've handled well.
4. Our hopes for the future.
5. Any other pleasant subject.

Let's ask one another, "What do you hear me saying?" and let's try to use as many of the other I COUNT—YOU COUNT skills that we can.

Either one of us can start.

Wrapping up

Here are some of the key points we've talked about during our last session.

1. Happiness can best be achieved when we adopt an attitude of I COUNT—YOU COUNT.

2. The I COUNT—YOU COUNT style is one in which we make maximum use of the communication skills we've learned in this program. We tune in, speak out, ask "What do you hear me saying?" and send I COUNT—YOU COUNT messages.

3. The I COUNT—YOU COUNT attitude can be summed up in the I COUNT—YOU COUNT message, "I may not like how you are behaving, but I respect your right to differ or to be angry at me. At the same time, I respect my right to differ and express anger with you. I also realize your anger and frustration often mean that you have a 'hurt inside.' "

4. The "I'm right—you're wrong," and "I win—you lose" attitudes produce new problems and greater marital strife. In contrast, the I COUNT—YOU COUNT attitude helps in problem solving and in resolving our differences.

5. With good communication, most of our problems can be worked out.

How have we done?

Now that we've shared many hours of reading together, discussing our personal problems, and holding I COUNT—YOU COUNT conversations, let's see how we've benefited by the program.

Has there been any noticeable improvement in our relationship? Have we put our couple power into good use?

In order to evaluate our progress, let's answer a series of ten questions. To do this, each of us will need a pen or pencil and a blank sheet of paper. Let's get this material now.

Now, let's write the numbers 1 through 10 in a vertical column on each of our individual sheets.

I'm going to read a series of statements. Our answers to the statements will give us a chance to evaluate how we are getting along *now* as compared with our behavior *before* we started the program.

After I read each statement, we will write the word **yes** or **no** next to the corresponding numbers on our sheets. We'll answer the statements independently of each other. Here are the statements:

1. **There have been positive changes between us as a result of our participation in the program.**

2. **We've developed a greater feeling of I COUNT—YOU COUNT.**

3. **We've been less tense and unpleasant with each other.**

4. **We are more accepting of each other.**

5. **We've been having more satisfactory experiences together.**

6. **We feel less ignored by each other.**

7. **We've been more open in expressing our feelings.**

8. **We've become less defensive.**

Let's write our answers to the next two questions on our sheets.

9. **If there have been changes between us since we've started the program, what have they been?**

10. **What aspects of the program have been most helpful?**

After we've written the answers, let's compare and discuss them.

TIME TO TALK

After the program is completed, what then?

This is your author-counselor speaking.

It is my sincere hope that you have found the program helpful and enriching. I hope that the positive changes will endure during the weeks, months, and years ahead. But regardless of how you may have benefited from the program, you can be sure that not all your problems will disappear. As we've stated before, life will never be all "bluebirds and pussywillows." You'll probably run into new difficulties and irritations that may arouse your hurt and angry feelings. You may slip back, from time to time, into old fight-flight patterns.

In the future, whenever a problem is brewing, it would be highly desirable to hold an I COUNT—YOU COUNT conversation rather than sweeping the problem under the rug or letting it fester inside. Holding an I COUNT—YOU COUNT conversation will give you an excellent chance to air your views

"What do you mean we're drifting apart? Can't we discuss this in the morning?"

in a constructive fashion. Again, let's remember to initiate the conversation by agreeing on the topic you wish to discuss and the time for it to be held.

Many problems can be averted by holding daily powwows or ten-and-ten letter dialogues. It would help immensely, if, every day, you thought of doing something that would please your partner—and then you went ahead and did it.

A good slogan to adopt is,

"A YOU COUNT a day keeps the marriage counselor away."

From time to time, it will be worthwhile to take a refresher course by rereading and following through on several of the sessions. Sessions Four, Five, Six, and Eight ("Tune in and speak out," "YOU COUNT," "Changing me—changing you," and "I COUNT—YOU COUNT") are particularly worth repeating.

In the same way that our car needs a regular five-thousand-mile checkup, our relationship will benefit from a periodic I COUNT—YOU COUNT booster. A good time to go through the program again is shortly after each wedding anniversary. It can be our special yearly gift to one another.

Above all, let's maintain an attitude of I COUNT—YOU COUNT in our daily living. If we do, we can't lose.

AFTERWORD

Suggestions for counselors and group leaders

Marriage: I COUNT—YOU COUNT is primarily a self-help book. It is designed mainly for the average man and woman who are getting along adequately but wish to improve their ability to communicate. However, as a marriage counselor, clergyman, social worker, or psychotherapist, you can easily adapt the program for use with couples who come to you for professional help.

If you have not had extensive experience in the counseling of couples, you will especially appreciate *Marriage: I COUNT—YOU COUNT* since it offers a ready-made, built-in marriage communication-counseling program.

Under your supervision, couples can experience *Marriage: I COUNT—YOU COUNT* concurrently with your counseling. They can take the program at home or they can share the book either before or immediately after their visits with you.

As their counselor, you should become familiar with the contents of the program. This will enable you to answer questions or help resolve any difficulties that may arise. You may even wish to start by sitting in on the first session with them. From time to time, you can review their I COUNT—YOU COUNT progress. You also can encourage them to follow through on the "between sessions" activities and suggestions.

The most valuable way of using the book, however, is by actually sitting in with the couple as they go through the program in your presence. Your comments and suggestions will help considerably in tailoring the program to their specific needs.

Using *Marriage: I COUNT—YOU COUNT* in the direct

counseling of couples has certain advantages that are often lacking in traditional marriage counseling. As you undoubtedly know, there are many frustrations and pitfalls in the counseling of unhappy couples. If a husband and wife are getting along poorly, their problems often resemble a large ball of string that has innumerable knots. While you are valiantly trying to untie one of the knots, the couple, with even stronger determination, may be busy tying three or four more.

Marriage: I COUNT—YOU COUNT offers an antidote to this exasperating phenomenon. When couples become absorbed in the program, they are committed to follow a planned sequence of activities. The structured nature of the program steers them away from destructive, "holy deadlock" entanglements and helps them explore their difficulties in a positive, constructive way. It also cuts down on wasted counseling hours.

The program presents the basic principles of good communication. Yet, at the same time, it enables couples to individualize these principles and apply them to their own lives. But no book can deal completely with the unique relationship inherent in each marriage. As a counselor, you'll be able to encourage couples to bring out their specific problems for discussion.

Marriage: I COUNT—YOU COUNT can supplement differing counseling approaches. If you are an adherent of Gestalt therapy, you can enrich the program by adding a variety of "here and now" exercises and experiences. If you are guided by Transactional Analysis, you can draw many parallels between the various communication styles presented in the book and the couples' specific parent-adult-child patterns. If you are inclined toward rational-emotive therapy, you undoubtedly will point out that I DON'T COUNT feelings often are self-induced. You then can suggest more rational "sentences" that will help couples feel less inadequate and less defensive.

Perhaps you may prefer a nondirective or consultant role in your counseling. If so, you can be of considerable help by mainly listening, reflecting feelings, or by answering questions and making suggestions.

In my own practice I try to apply an essentially I COUNT—YOU COUNT approach that is consistent with the principles and communication skills taught in the program. I let couples know that I accept their differences. I listen attentively. I ask, "What do you hear me saying?" and "Do you mean. . ?" questions. I give positive strokes and urge the expression of I COUNT—YOU COUNT messages. At times, I issue bad-mood warnings and encourage couples to do likewise. My comments are not only intended as therapeutic aids but also serve as examples that couples can emulate.

Here are a few sample I COUNT—YOU COUNT counselor statements:

I COUNT messages

Connie, there was a noticeable quiver to your voice when you were speaking to Harold. Could you tune in to your voice? What is your quiver saying? Could you express it in an I COUNT message?

Mike, you've just said to Helen that she was self-centered and showed no consideration for your needs. Could you say what you want to say, again? But this time try using I COUNT messages.

I feel annoyed when you repeatedly come late to our appointments. *I wish* you'd make a greater effort to get here on time.

YOU COUNT messages

I can understand why you feel so rejected when Ron leaves "for an hour" and then comes home four hours later. But, Doris, do you think that calling him "immature" and "totally irresponsible" is helping him change his behavior?

Bill, I can see your point of view. I can see why you feel so defensive about Sarah's behavior. But why don't you sit back awhile and think about what Sarah's been going through. Try putting yourself in her shoes and try seeing things from her viewpoint, even though you may not agree with her. When you do, try to express your feelings by using YOU COUNT messages.

I COUNT, "hurt inside" messages

I know that I would feel awfully hurt inside if somebody stopped talking to me. Is this the way you feel when Doris gives you the silent treatment?

Mark, I know you're damn angry at Eloise. But beneath your anger you are hurting. You have some emotional pain. Could you tell Eloise what's hurting you, what you are frustrated about?

"What do you hear me saying?"

I hear you saying, Sue, that despite your difficulties with Bart, you're beginning to treat each other more like people who count and that things are really looking up between you. Do I read you right?

Kate, I'm not sure that you are listening to Tom. What do you hear him saying?

Revealing one's own inadequacies (nondefensiveness)

I really goofed up when I called you Joan instead of Jackie. For a moment I got you mixed up with another woman. I feel sort of foolish. I hope you'll forgive me.

Accepting differences

Your husband enjoys the excitement of investing in the stock market, while you're a conservative, financially. A six percent savings account is good enough for you. Do you think that your viewpoint is right and his is ridiculous? Or do you see it mainly as a matter of legitimate differences between you?

Asking partner to look at her or himself

Rather than blaming Sarah for the embarrassment you've suffered, what do *you* think you've contributed to the difficulties? And what do *you* think you can do to improve the situation?

Commenting on body language

I noticed, Pat, when you were listening to Cliff, you had a frown on your face. You still do. What do you think your frown is saying? Could you put it into words? Could you express it in an I COUNT message?

Positive strokes

I think your suggestion is a stroke of genius.

It's wonderful to see you so happy. You seem to be really enjoying one another's company.

You look as if you are very appreciative of what Debby just did for you. Do you think it would be nice to let Debby know how you feel?

The intended and the accompanying message

Counselor: Your words, the message you wish to convey to Pete, is that you wish he would stop eating so loudly. But there's a lot of music accompanying your wish. I wonder what it is?

Pete: Yeah. The music I'm picking up is "You dumb hick, when will you ever learn?"

Bad-mood warnings

I'm feeling distressed over a phone call I just received. Give me a few minutes to get my bearings. Then I can give you my undivided attention.

Bill, you seem to be in a bad mood right now. Why don't you tune in to it and let Linda know how you feel?

The pitcher and the glass

Counselor: What Liz is trying to get across to you is her wish that you be firmer about having the children in by 10:30. This is what's coming out of her pitcher. But I wonder what's going into your glass? How are you reacting emotionally?

Carl: What my glass is picking up from Liz is, "You've goofed again." I feel that I'm in trouble again, that I'm being accused of being a lousy father. So I back away. I'd rather not be involved in this problem at all. Let Liz handle the kids.

I COUNT—YOU COUNT messages

Connie: I get so damn mad when you come home late without phoning or letting me know. I feel like choking you when you show up so late.

Jack: What are you so angry about? For God's sake, can't you simmer down and talk to me calmly?

Connie: Calmly, my eye. I can't win no matter what I do. First you urge me to express my feelings, but when I do, you shush me up.

Counselor: Jack, it seems as if you are putting Connie in a bind. I wonder if you could express your feelings to Connie in the form of an I COUNT—YOU COUNT message?

Jack: Yes. I see what you mean. (YOU COUNT) Connie, I can understand why you get so upset at me when I come home late. I should phone you. (I COUNT) But I'm not trying to supress your emotions. I don't enjoy your yelling at me one bit. But I still would rather have you come out with your feelings than give me the silent treatment.

Here are several other specific suggestions that can be of help.

1. An average session takes between one and two hours. If you are operating on a fifty minute, or a one-hour session schedule, the *Marriage: I COUNT—YOU COUNT* session can be concluded during the next visit. Or, if you prefer, the couple can finish it by themselves, in an adjoining room or at home.

2. In order to keep up with the couple's discussions and activities, you should use your own copy of the book and read along with them.

3. If either the husband or wife has difficulty reading his or her role, you can pinch hit and share in the reading. Discussions and shared activities, however, are to be done by the couples themselves.

4. Remind *each* partner to discuss each of the questions that appear in the question sections.

5. Encourage the less communicative partner to speak more. Urge the more talkative one to listen more.

6. During discussion periods, couples often will turn toward you and speak to you, instead of to each other. When this occurs, urge them to address one another. Also, suggest that they use the direct pronouns, "you" and "I," instead of alluding to one another as "she" and "he."

7. Press the "red-alert button" and ask them to stop the argument if you sense that the couple is becoming embroiled in a fight-flight brawl. Later, they can elect to continue the discussion, providing they conduct a "What do you hear me saying?" type of conversation.

8. Stress the positive. If possible, end each section on a constructive note.

Although *Marriage: I COUNT—YOU COUNT* is designed for individual marriages, it can easily be adapted for groups of couples. It has been used, with gratifying results, by small groups of two to six couples during group counseling sessions and at marital enrichment workshops.

Once couples discover that their communication difficulties and marital frustrations are not unique or abnormal, they enjoy working in a group setting. Couples help one another through mutual support. They share experiences, accept each other's expression of feelings, make constructive suggestions, and in general, elevate each other's I COUNT feelings.

Group leaders can either be trained counselors or couples who enjoy helping others. A husband and wife team is most effective when they are open, warm, and sensitive to the needs and feelings of others. They should have the capacity to tune in to their own feelings and disclose them to the group.

Many groups find it congenial to operate without one set leader. Individual couples can take turns leading each section. Or the group might conduct entirely leaderless meetings.

Marriage: I COUNT—YOU COUNT can be presented in several ways. The usual procedure is to have couples sit next to each other as the group arranges itself in a circle. Each section then is read aloud and passed from one person to another. Discussions and activities either can be confined to each of the individual couples or can be open for group discusion.

Another method is to have each couple go through the program privately in separate rooms. At the end of each of the eight sessions the couples assemble in one room and discuss their reactions to the session.

Couples at marital weekend retreats may not have the time to complete the entire program. Instead, they can select several sessions of the book and follow through on them in either one of the two ways described above.

As you become more familiar with *Marriage: I COUNT—YOU COUNT,* I'm sure you'll introduce your own innovative modifications of the program.

Additional Readings on Communication for Couples

1. Bach, George R., and Wyden, Peter. *The Intimate Enemy.* New York: William Morrow and Co. 1969.

2. Bosco, Antoinette. *Marriage Encounter.* St. Meinrad, Indiana: Abbey Press. 1973.

3. Clinebell, Howard J., and Clinebell, Charlotte H. *The Intimate Marriage.* New York: Harper and Row. 1971.

4. Herrigan, Jackie, and Herrigan, Jeff. *Loving Free.* New York: Ballantine Books. 1974.

5. Lessor, L. Richard. *Love and Marriage and Trading Stamps.* Niles, Illinois: Argus Communications. 1971.

6. Mace, David R., and Mace, Vera. *We Can Have Better Marriages.* Nashville: Abingdon Press. 1974.

7. Miller, Sherod; Nunnally, Elam W.; Wachman, Daniel B.; and Bragman, Ronald. *The Minnesota Couples Communication Program.* Minneapolis: 1972.

8. Powell, John, S.J. *Why Am I Afraid to Tell You Who I Am?* Niles, Illinois: Argus Communications. 1969.

9. Satir, Virginia. *Peoplemaking.* Palo Alto: Science and Behavior Books. 1972.

10. Smith, Gerald Walker, and Phillips, Alice J. *Couple Therapy.* New York: Collier Books. 1973.

11. Wilke, Richard B. *Tell Me Again, I'm Listening.* Nashville: Abingdon Press. 1973.